HOW TO RAISE HAPPY
NEUROFABULOUS CHILDREN

of related interest

The Strengths-Based Guide to Supporting Autistic Children
A Positive Psychology Approach to Parenting
Claire O'Neill
ISBN 978 1 83997 215 7
eISBN 978 1 83997 216 4

Parenting Rewired
How to Raise a Happy Autistic Child in a Very Neurotypical World
Danielle Punter and Charlotte Chaney
ISBN 978 1 83997 072 6
eISBN 978 1 83997 073 3

Nurturing Your Autistic Young Person
A Parent's Handbook to Supporting Newly Diagnosed Teens and Pre-Teens
Cathy Wassell
Illustrated by Eliza Fricker
Foreword by Emily Burke
ISBN 978 1 83997 111 2
eISBN 978 1 83997 112 9

The Family Experience of PDA
An Illustrated Guide to Pathological Demand Avoidance
Eliza Fricker
Illustrated by Eliza Fricker
Foreword by Ruth Fidler
ISBN 978 1 78775 677 9
eISBN 978 1 78775 678 6

How to Raise
Happy Neurofabulous Children

A PARENTS' GUIDE

Katy Elphinstone

Illustrated by Matt Friedman

Jessica Kingsley Publishers
London and Philadelphia

Jessica Kingsley Publishers London and Philadelphia
First published in Great Britain in 2024 by Jessica Kingsley Publishers
An imprint of John Murray Press

2

A CIP catalogue record for this title is available from the British Library
and the Library of Congress

ISBN 978 1 80501 092 0
eISBN 978 1 80501 093 7

Printed and bound in the United States by Integrated Books International

Jessica Kingsley Publishers' policy is to use papers that are natural, renewable
and recyclable products and made from wood grown in sustainable forests.
The logging and manufacturing processes are expected to conform to the
environmental regulations of the country of origin.

Jessica Kingsley Publishers
Carmelite House
50 Victoria Embankment
London EC4Y 0DZ

www.jkp.com

John Murray Press
Part of Hodder & Stoughton Ltd
An Hachette Company

Contents

Author's note

This book started its life as a list of personal reminders jotted down in a notebook. I wrote it as two lists: what clearly worked, and what didn't work, in raising my kids – one of whom is neurodivergent, as am I (we're both autistic).

The two headings were written at the top of each page, in thick black pen. 'Do' and 'Don't'. I consulted my list quite frequently when going about my daily life as a parent: 'Oh, now *what* did I write about what to do in this scenario?' Very often, the pause I took for consulting my notes meant me taking a very helpful 'step back' from the situation. And that was even before I knew what they said!

The information I gathered was, at first, based on my everyday life as a parent. But this hands-on experience was quickly accompanied by a huge amount of research and reading.

I chatted with, interviewed, and gained valuable information (often in the form of polls and questionnaires) from hundreds of neurodivergent adults and teenagers, many of whom are disabled in other ways too, and a number of whom are non-speaking. These wonderful people – to whom I extend my enormous thanks and gratitude – have consistently, patiently answered my questions (however apparently illogical!) about their lives, their feelings about specific things, what they remember about their childhood (the positives *and* the negatives), and how they think they've been affected later in life by their childhood experiences.

At some point along this journey, it dawned on me that the information I had gathered could be useful for others, too. And so this book was born.

Introduction

As parents, we want to understand our children – to connect with them – and for them to be happy. But this path is often fraught with obstacles. A great deal of what's coming at us (and often, everything we've ever known) tells us to do things in certain ways. And yet worryingly we may see, with our own eyes, that these ways really aren't working – neither for ourselves nor our children.

When you're right in the thick of things, it's hard – if not downright impossible – to see the wood for the trees. And let's face it, when things are going wrong for our children, we're often in the thickest of thickets! This is why, within the pages of this book, I focus on the little steps – the 'forward march' – in the form of bite-sized tips. Things that feel actually doable and don't (usually, anyway) make me go, 'Aarrgh!' and run the other way.

The steps, however seemingly insignificant in themselves, fall in the context of a bigger journey. A journey which leads (with any luck!) to higher ground, with lovely places where we can enjoy views over the whole wood.

A lot of the tips are relevant for all ages but, overall, they're intended for younger children (from around two to twelve years old).

And just a heads up, before we start, that the tips within these pages are *never* meant to be followed in any strict or systematic way. Indeed, they couldn't really be, as they're often specific to certain situations, as and when they might come up (and some of them might never come up for you – depending on your living and/or economic situation, on the constellation and setup of your family, on your child's preferences, on their support needs, and so on).

All the suggestions are meant as entirely optional, to try out (or not!) in whatever 'mix and match' works for you and your family – and that you feel physically able to do without wiping yourself out completely.

CHAPTER 1
Basics

The first and greatest resource of a parent is a deeply loving heart. And the second one is a vastly open mind!

This chapter contains some broader ideas which might, I hope, start creating a picture of how we might best help our neurodivergent children in this world. I've included both the obvious and the less obvious – so forgive me if some of these seem like complete no-brainers to you. In the rest of the book, the tips get more specific (and you can skip straight to those, if you prefer).

Do...

☐ Believe in your child and love them *just the way they are*. There are more tips on ways to do this, and how to show it to them, in Chapter 11, 'Emotions' and Chapter 5, 'Friendship'.
☐ Make sure your child/children know they don't have to *be* something specific, nor *do* something specific, to earn your admiration.

- ☐ Take your child's interests, feelings, views, and worries seriously. Take time to listen.
- ☐ Use direct speech and honesty as a general principle within the family. More on all this in Chapter 6, 'Communication'.
- ☐ Try to respect the preferences expressed by your child wherever possible, even if they don't make sense to you.
- ☐ Support your child in situations when they're put down or sold short by others, even other grown-ups – *even* ones in positions of authority.
- ☐ Wherever possible, help your child out when they ask you to. Do this even if you don't understand why, or you personally don't think what they are asking for help with is important, or you reckon they could do it for themselves if they tried. More in Chapter 7, 'Learning and School'.
- ☐ Make sure your child gets enough downtime, and opportunities to follow their own interests. More about this in Chapter 3, 'Downtime and Hobbies'.
- ☐ Choose your battles. Consider your priorities and decide which specific areas you really need to be firm in. This will leave you free to be flexible on other areas you find less important.
- ☐ Make it clear that kindness and consideration are top priorities (parents are in a great position to lead by example).
- ☐ Be aware that if there are any unspoken, unresolved conflicts in their surrounding environment, your child is likely to unconsciously be picking up on them (and, most likely, manifesting this in their behaviour).
- ☐ Know that it's okay to have disagreements. Living without any conflict would not only be impossible, but (I think) undesirable too. And it's great training for settling disputes constructively. More on this in Chapter 6, 'Communication'.
- ☐ Say how you feel, keeping it brief and relevant to the situation – yes, even if you're cross or tired! This will make it much easier for your child to understand how you're acting, and why.

If you see your child interpreting blame or reproach when you neutrally express negative feelings in their presence, openly reassure them it's no one's fault. (But more about what to do if you're actually feeling quite annoyed with someone can be found in Chapter 6, 'Communication').[1]

☐ If you're cross and having a reaction to something someone did, instead of blaming them or assassinating their character (the latter being my own particular weakness), try saying, 'I'm so angry with so-and-so! I think I'm having a big reaction to what they did/said.'

We've got a little doll made from an empty kitchen paper roll, with two bottle tops for eyes and cotton wool for hair. He sits on the shelf and is called 'No one'.

He was made by the kids, following some discussion ending in, 'It's no one's fault... Only...who's "no one"?'

And now he exists we feel very sorry for him...as it's always his fault.

☐ Be aware that if you give too many options too frequently, your child may be saying 'no' (or 'yes'!) to things by default. The volume of decision-making about small things may just be overwhelming them.

☐ Try not to be ruled by 'what people think' – keeping a careful eye out for motivations such as social embarrassment, other people's expectations, or conformism for its own sake.

☐ Lead by example. Children, as my mum says, are like sponges. They absorb and then (sometimes after a little time has passed) give out what they've seen/felt happening around them. Speaking from my own experience, this phenomenon can be extremely disconcerting. Below are a couple of (I hope) realistic examples.

Generosity and empathy: in the supermarket, 'Ooh look, Auntie Holly loves mustard-flavoured crisps – let's buy her a packet!'; seeing buskers on the street, 'I love hearing music out of doors,' and putting (or helping/letting the child put) some money in the hat; leaving tips in cafés – little kids often love putting coins in the cup; and so on.

Saying 'please', 'thank you' and similar: well, I think this one's fairly obvious. And sometimes afterwards – quite genuinely! – adding, 'Aw, that was so lovely of that woman to let us go in front of her' (or whatever it was).

☐ Don't make promises to your child you aren't close to 100 per cent certain you can keep. (I only say 'close to' because...well, *anything* could happen, up to and including meteor strikes.)
☐ If your child breaks something, focus on the person and not the object.

'Darling, it was only the silly Wedgwood vase. Are *you* okay?'

☐ Try to give health warnings non-dramatically, as your child might be prone to developing real phobias around things.
☐ Live in the moment. Take things slowly – *enjoy!*

Don't...

☐ Don't blame your family members (or yourself – or indeed, anyone). Ever. For anything. It's not logical, as everything always happens for reasons.
☐ Avoid using criticism. When you're tempted to, examine what your expectations are and what outcome you're hoping for. More on this in Chapter 6, 'Communication'.

☐ Never throw out or give away anyone's possessions (including clothes, however worn out!) without asking permission first.

☐ Don't tell anecdotes about your children (no, not even positive ones!) without first making sure they're happy with it.

☐ Try not to make light of things that are very important to your child. If it's big to them, it's big.

☐ Don't ever poke fun at a child for being wildly enthusiastic or exuberant. Instead, feel free to join them in their joy.

About jokes

When using humour, as a rule make sure you range yourself alongside your child/children/family (or all children, or all people, depending on the situation), rather than making jokes that are at anyone's expense. Even if they're funny ones.

☐ Avoid pushing, or even encouraging, gender roles. Let your child act and dress in a way that makes them feel relaxed.[2]

☐ As much as you can, avoid exposing your child to people who dislike or disapprove of them and who don't appreciate their qualities (they'll anyway get enough of that in their lives to fill *that* space, believe me!).

☐ Don't make your child do things they've expressed a strong wish not to. Children challenge themselves, and branch out, when the drive comes from within.[3] More on this in Chapter 7, 'Learning and School'.

☐ Don't say 'don't' (yes, I know! Blush!). Instead, try clearly stated rules (which apply to everyone), for example, 'Shoes off at the door.' And give information in a firm manner, for example 'This is a very steep slope' or 'That tea is scalding hot.'

An unexpected side-effect of saying 'don't' is that children hear the *expectation* in what you say (i.e. you're asking them not to do it, but your expectation is they probably will). So, you say, 'Don't touch the oven', and they promptly do so.

There can an issue about clarity as well. 'Put your shoes on the shoe rack', is a clear instruction, while 'Don't drop your shoes in the middle of the floor', is not.

☐ And finally, don't worry if things go wrong, and you realize afterwards that what you did or said was less than helpful – okay, or totally disastrous, as the case may be. A family without mess-ups and mistakes would be no family at all!

CHAPTER 2
At Home

Be it ever so humble, there's no place like home.
John Payne, 1823

Home is a place children need to feel safe, relaxed, and nurtured – and this becomes *especially* important for neurodivergent ones. Neurodivergent people (whether autistic, ADHD, or other) invariably experience higher-than-average levels of tension (even fear!) in our daily lives. This means we need *plenty* of time in our cosy, familiar environments where we can de-stress, unwind, and recharge our batteries.

Below are a few tips, some of which you'll be familiar with – but one or two of which I hope may be useful.

Just a note before I begin, though, that you mustn't start hyperventilating while reading this, thinking, 'How can I *ever* provide all this?' The answer is, you don't have to. No one could. Each point you don't greet with a resounding 'can do!' can be walked right past. Perhaps see it as a bit like shopping for comfy T-shirts in a clothes store, rather than learning verbs for a test.

☐ Create a space or spaces for your child (a 'nest') with a selection of toys, books, and so on. They might like soft blankets and cushions, and low or warm-coloured lighting (or different options for lighting they can choose between).

☐ Especially if you live in a city and have no garden or park nearby, have some house plants around the place (if practical). They provide oxygen, greenery, and a calm 'feel'.

☐ Try to be as minimalist as you can, while keeping the gear you need for your and your child's interests. Your child will benefit from things being reasonably orderly, but please, do *not* worry if this feels like it would finish you off – there are other things, like love and connection, that are much more important.

> To quote an autistic child: 'When things are untidy and everything's out of place, it's like there's noise in the room.'

☐ Try doing clear-outs together of your child's space, perhaps on a yearly basis (their needs and interests change over time). Ideally, your child can be 'in charge' as it's very important they're happy with the process. Lots of snack breaks, breathers, and/ or cups of tea or coffee (for the parent) may be needed during this process. Note: it can work quite well to clear out everything from the room/space in question, piling it all just outside e.g. in the corridor. Then, it's a question for your child of considering – when it comes to each item – what they want (to go back in their space again), rather than what they don't want.

☐ Spend time together (this can be in a companionable silence, there's no need to talk a lot) in your communal spaces – either working on a project together or just alongside each other.

☐ If you've the energy for it, play some family games like cards, board games, Twister (if you're agile), charades, consequences, acting games or guessing games – or any other shared activity that your family enjoys. Doing this as a regular thing can be nice, perhaps before a family movie, for example on a Friday evening.

Sensory stuff

Differences in sensory processing are a foundation part of neurodivergence (whether it's autism, ADHD, or other).

Hyper-receptivity to sensory input, very common in neurodivergent people, means our chances of sensory overload are high – although this can be an advantage as well, as it brings with it the capacity to be aware of ambient nuances, beauty, and subtlety.

Most of us need to spend significant time in uncrowded, calm environments that are pleasant to the senses (this is, in part, why natural environments can be so beneficial), or at least to have these available should the need arise.

At times, on the other hand, we can be 'sensory seeking' (*also* motivated by an instinct towards self-regulation and balance – and which can involve huge enjoyment for us!). Your child might love bouncing on beds, loud music, crashing waves, spinning fast on roundabouts, and even rollercoaster rides.

A lot of the harder-to-manage behaviours shown by neurodivergent children are down to sensory discomfort and/or overwhelm.[4] This happens when a) things get too much, and b) we aren't in control of them (an important aspect that *very* often gets overlooked).

Thankfully, there are lots of ways to maximize the positives, and minimize the negatives, of our sensory experiences.

To avoid being overwhelmed:

☐ Use dimmer switches, low-output bulbs, and/or have different options for lighting. Avoid fluorescent lighting and LED bulbs.
☐ Have comfortable spaces within your home where it's not too

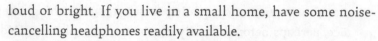

loud or bright. If you live in a small home, have some noise-cancelling headphones readily available.

☐ Give your child some control over their environment, and especially over their personal spaces, as early as possible – have light switches or lamps low enough for them to click on and off, blankets and cushions in places they can reach them, blinds or curtains they can pull on a cord to open or close, and so on.

☐ Observe for signs of overwhelm, and let (and/or help) your child leave or change any environments they're unhappy in.

☐ Let your child wear clothes they find comfortable (and cut the labels out of them).

It can feel like real torture for an autistic child to wear uncomfortable clothes (we're not exaggerating, I promise!).

A few things lots of neurodivergent people swear by are hoodies (fleece-lined in winter, thin and soft in summer), soft cotton tracksuit bottoms or leggings, and no-seam socks (preferably bought a size too large, as socks shrink a bit when washed).

☐ If you have any views out of windows that show sky or greenery, see if you can make some comfy spaces where those views are easily visible.

☐ If possible, have curtains or shutters to regulate light, or if there's a lack of privacy indoors when it's dark outside.

When sensory seeking, on the other hand:

☐ Provide lots of sensory play for young children using sand, water, earth, playdough or clay, materials and fabrics, art supplies (e.g. large rolls of paper and large bottles of washable paint). If you have space out-of-doors, this is ideal for this kind of play. Otherwise, large oilcloths can be useful for covering floors and tables.

- Show your kids how to make their own playdough, using white flour, salt, water, and food colourings. (Tip: add the colours to the water in a glass; it works best, and it looks lovely!) Besides being a great way to learn about mixing colours, the dough feels and smells nice, and it's often played with for hours afterwards (then store it in an airtight bag in the fridge).
- If you can, provide lots of creative, sensory, hands-on experience just in everyday living. Even very small children can help with baking, cooking, and gardening (don't be too fussy about the results!).
- Some children love baths as sensory experiences. More on these in Chapter 9, 'Health, Hygiene, and Fitness'.
- Your child might need a space in the house that allows for free movement such as spinning around, jumping, or listening/dancing to music (note: this can also be done using headphones).
- It can also help to have opportunities in the house for hanging or being upside-down, or safely climbing up onto things.
- For children who like/need deep pressure, perhaps try out a heavy vest or pendant, or a large watch, cuff, or bracelet that has some tightness but isn't uncomfortable.
- Some children love chewing or biting on things. If your child does, there is some great 'chewellery' available (chewable jewellery) – just make sure it's safe and from a trusted supplier.
- Natural oils can be a great way to make an environment pleasant and reassuring. In our family, a few drops of lavender oil make us all feel settled, familiar, and relaxed – and it's great for when we go elsewhere, for example, on holiday, to make a place feel more like home. (Note: when using a new product, oil, or fragrance in the house, make sure beforehand there aren't any adverse/allergic reactions to it.)
- Some kids may use food for sensory balance and/or reassurance (e.g. crunchy, spicy, strong, salty, sugary, or a specific foodstuff). While this *can* be positive, habitually using food for emotional

reassurance can become problematic – so if your child is doing this, maybe a) look for some alternatives, and b) work on reducing anxiety levels. Lots more about emotional self-regulatory habits (or 'stims') can be found in Chapter 11, 'Emotions', in the section 'Stimming'.

Hyposensitivity

While neurodivergent people are generally *hyper*sensitive to sensory input, there may be times when we show little or no reaction when exposed to sensory stimuli (even painful ones). This is known as '*hypo*sensitivity'. Note: we may have notable hypersensitivities in certain areas while almost entirely lacking sensitivity in others.[5] Whether we're sensitive to things or not can also, at times, depend on our environment and anxiety levels in the moment.

Routines, predictability, and flexibility

Neurodivergent people tend to have a strong need – and in some cases, a strong desire as well – for structure and routine in our lives.

A reasonable degree of structure, routine, and habit is natural to humans. It makes sense logistically, and it makes us feel safe – but this attachment to routine can grow arms and legs, manifesting itself (especially in autistics and people with obsessive compulsive disorder – OCD) as a desire for minute control, obsession with details, and adherence to inflexible and burdensome routines – and, potentially, meltdowns or shutdowns when unpredictable things happen. In those with attention deficit hyperactivity disorder (ADHD), on the other hand, it may be less about craving structure than running the risk of completely falling apart without it.

So why this heavy reliance, and why the dire consequences we, as neurodivergent people, may suffer when our routines fail us?

Being this attached or dependent upon routines, and/or unable to function without them, I think comes out of an overall feeling of being a bit lost in the world, usually with very few reference points – and no map.

> I see it a bit like after a shipwreck. At first, you're flailing about in the water, thinking you're probably going to drown. But then, you see a beam floating nearby. You manage, with some difficulty, to get to it, and then...you cling on, very tightly! You're not drowning any more (not quite – but it's precarious). Then you notice some other floating bits and bobs, and realize you can reach those too – so you reel them in. Yay, a raft!
> This is how I feel about my routines and fixed habits. And, if you tried to get me to abandon my raft and get back into the sea again? Well, I think you can probably imagine the scene.

Autistic people may therefore construct ways we can control our environment,[6] or else, in instances when we're powerless, we may mentally dissociate (withdraw) or melt down. For those with ADHD, on the other hand, there may be chaotic/muddled thinking, changeableness (the butterfly effect – trying different things), avoidance, and studiously not-thinking-about-the-future (future, what future?!). [7]

The key lies in building up our children's trust, both in us and in the universe. If we can get those feelings of precariousness and apprehension to abate, the need for restrictive regimes (whether self-imposed or having to be imposed by others) will gradually do so too. And in its place will grow more flexible and joyful routines, rituals, and habits – and more adventurousness. That's the plan, anyway!

Happy routines and habits

☐ Have lots of pleasant, regular habits in your lives, and give your child some say in what and when they are (or at least check they're happy with the plan). Examples could be: movies together in the evening after dinner; a cup of hot chocolate with marshmallows at a café on Saturdays; board games after lunch if it's rainy outside. And so on.

☐ Make as many things in your lives as possible be ones that you and your child enjoy and want to do. (If, proportionally, most things in a child's life are hard and anxiety-provoking, it stands to reason their feelings of apprehension will mount.)

> If I say to my kid, 'Hey, let's go for an ice cream – okay with you if we leave in ten minutes?' this might elicit a rather different reaction from if I say, 'We're going to the doctor's for your medical check-up. You've got ten minutes to get ready.'
>
> To quote an autistic person, 'Things I don't find scary in any way don't need to be all planned and predictable.'
>
> And, 'If I really want to do something, there can be quite a lot of challenges and unknowns in there!'

Planning, calendars, and lists

☐ Make sure to give your children a good few minutes' warning before going out, or for anything else that requires changing activity. This helps mitigate any feelings of precariousness and being blown about like a leaf on the wind.

☐ Have an analogue or digital clock on your wall or counter in a visible position. One that doesn't tick.

☐ If plans change, make sure you tell your child what's happening. Even when very little, they prefer to know what's going on.

☐ At breakfast each morning, or in another appropriate moment and setting depending on your family's habits, spend a few moments talking together about the overall plans for the day (or week – perhaps for an older child, or if plans are varying a lot). Choose a moment when your child is happy to do this with you. If they're not that interested, keep it to the absolute basics. If, on the other hand, they asked you about it or want to know more, then you can make it more detailed and involving. And if anything you're saying is obviously provoking anxiety, resistance, or withdrawal, you may want to revise your plans accordingly.

□ Be prepared and patient if your child keeps randomly asking questions about what's happening, even if you've already told them five times.

□ In some cases, it can be handy to use a wall or picture calendar with/for your child to provide an overview of what's happening. Note: this can be done with pictures, emojis, colours, and so on as well as text.

□ But (big 'but' here!) *if* you decide to take the calendar route, keep it nice and relaxed – and flexible! Otherwise, there's a risk of overwhelming your child and/or making them feel trapped. Plus, if it's done in a rigid way, a child could reasonably start thinking that if you deviated from the calendar in any way, the sky may fall in.

When creating schedules, planners, and calendars, it's important to find the balance between what's useful, what's fun and pleasurable, and what just causes more anxiety.

□ Only use a calendar of this kind if your child likes it and *they* feel they're benefitting from it (if they don't want it, don't force it on them).

Whose calendar?

Collaboration, and listening to your child, are of huge importance. For me, there would be an enormous difference between a calendar full of items I chose most of myself (or at least had a real say in), and a calendar made up of someone else's expectations of me.

If children feel forced into things, it will, sooner or later, trigger their 'counterwill' (a natural feature of human psychology often overlooked when we're trying to get kids to do things).[8]

☐ Some find a 'flexible list' approach useful, to keep some (flexible!) tabs on what's happening next. Together, you can make a list of optional activities and/or tasks for certain days or timeslots. This can work quite well for AuDHDers (those with ADHD *and* autism), who combine anxiety and hesitancy to try new things with getting bored quickly when things are always the same.

Flexibility

It's good if we can manage to get our children used to different places, people, and things, in as safe and pleasurable a way as possible. Some suggestions for ways to do this are in the following tips.

☐ Try injecting some novelty into routines or allow for creativity within them. The novel or creative elements can be chosen by your children or collaboratively.

We stop before our music lessons at a café where there's table football. We always leave enough time for a match (okay, and for my coffee). We have to leave the house a few minutes earlier, but somehow the 'fun relaxed thing' in the schedule helps reduce any nervousness around the lesson, and whether we've practised enough!

☐ If changes need to be made to a child's routines that they're not quite sold on, do lots of checking in (with self and child!) to make sure it's going okay. If the process is causing distress or dissociation, it's probably best to backtrack, if possible, and re-group.

☐ When it comes to introducing the idea of flexibility because of accommodating others' needs, bear in mind a child may be happier, at first, about accommodating (for example) their pet turtle's needs, than (for example) their younger sibling's.

☐ Show your child your own flexibility, especially around their wishes and preferences, wherever you can practically do so.

But won't my child expect me to be flexible all the time, if I'm flexible sometimes?

Well – strangely, not really! The more flexible you are with your child about most things, the more likely it is your child will take in their stride the things where you have little choice and really have to be rigid about. It's a direct (if rather counter-intuitive) correlation that I've – slightly to my amazement at first – observed first-hand. I believe this is because greater autonomy, about most things, brings about more equanimity, and therefore a greater openness to others' views and ways of doing things (when it's necessary).

Helping in the house

But only if your child is able, and up for it! Having your kids help out in the house is great – but only if it's not at the expense of anyone's wellbeing or of your relationship with your child.

☐ Let your child 'help out' when they're little. The biggest hack to having a child who's willing to help is having had the time, leeway, energy, and patience to let them help from the moment they first wanted to (okay, though perhaps one wouldn't describe it as 'help' exactly).

☐ Accept all offered and forthcoming help cheerfully. Let your children do as much or as little as they feel up to, without critique or pressurizing them into doing more, or doing things better (as if you do, they may well think, 'I'll just keep my head down next time').

☐ Rather than faithfully sticking to tasks at your child's ability level, go instead for tasks you think they'll enjoy doing (obviously depending on what the risks are). I know one child who, astonishingly, loves tidying up cutlery drawers, finding great satisfaction in it.

☐ Try offering choices, for example, 'The animals need feeding, and the table needs to be laid for breakfast. Shall we do one task each? You choose which you prefer – I don't mind.'

☐ Although sometimes it makes a lot of sense to assign specific chores to people, it's also great to have some flexibility around who does what in the house. The more different tasks your child does (maybe starting with doing them together), the less likely it is to get boring for them, and the more equipped they become for gradually managing more things on their own.

☐ Tasks can be a *lot* more fun when done together – so when you're doing things, go ahead and ask your kids if they want to be involved. But remember, you're asking them about their preference here – so don't apply *any* pressure or persuasion if they show unwilling or are busy.

Working together could include any tasks, but a few examples are: cleaning the car, hanging/folding laundry, cooking, tidying out drawers, wrapping presents, sorting out the pens and throwing out the ones that don't work, or sharpening the pencils.

Your kids learn a lot from doing things with you, plus you get a chance to be together – perhaps putting on some music to listen to, or a talking book, if you both like that.

☐ But if you really *want* them to do a task with you because you genuinely need help with it, you can use a more direct style. You could start with, 'I need help here.' Children – especially neuro-divergent ones – like to know the score up front (is this a request you're making of them because you need help, or are you just asking if they feel like it?).

☐ If your kid refuses to do a task that you ask them to do, it's best to take it on the chin. It's fairly pointless pushing the issue, as this usually only causes them either to dig their heels in (and not do it) or else feel deeply resentful (while they do it as ineffectively as possible).

Over time I've learned that, if the focus is on a) the enjoyable, and b) being in this together, it's fine to be flexible (resigned?) about what doesn't get done by my kids. In fact, I've often seen with hindsight that I was asking my children to do things they weren't up for at their age.

☐ Try, if it feels appropriate, to get into the habit of regularly hand-ing out small tasks to your family members – going with those you know they don't mind doing, and aren't too complex, e.g. 'Could you get us three glasses out of the cupboard?' and (per-haps to a different child if you have more than one of them) 'And could you fill up the water jug?'

☐ Don't give neurodivergent people/children lots of instructions all at once, as our operating system will do a 'bluescreen' on us. If your child's up for doing a task, give instructions one at a time – or, for older children, write them out as a list. Note: make your wording concise. You could use some emojis and/or quickly sketched illustrations, too, if you like.

Written tasks can work better than spoken instructions. This is certainly the case for us. My son's perfectly happy to work through tasks on a list (I draw a little box next to them for him to check off once they're done), but if we try talking about what tasks there are to do around the house, we get in a complete tangle (not helped by how hard I find it asking for 'help', and him picking up on my tension big-time).

☐ If your child is flatly against doing anything at all, try (for a while at least) to only ask them to do fun, optional, small tasks, for example, 'Do you want to pick the pasta shape we're having?', or 'Hey, could you squoosh some cream onto those meringues?'

☐ Don't give rewards for doing chores, beyond logical things like 'When we've cleaned up, we can go out,' or 'Just as soon as you guys have laid the table, we can eat.' (Extrinsic rewarding can be problematic.[9] I'll come back to this in Chapter 6 on 'Communication'.)

☐ If reminders become necessary, avoid starting to plead or criticize. One-worders can be good, for example, 'Shoes' or, 'Table' (pointing).

☐ Calling small ad-hoc family meetings can work quite well, for example, when one person is getting overwhelmed with tasks. You can start, 'Right, everyone. This is what needs doing...' On a bit of paper, then write things out (some silly drawings or emojis can work nicely here, too). And, with any luck, the kids might come out with 'I'll lay out breakfast!', 'I'll feed the animals!', and so on.

☐ No need to offer suggestions or corrections when your child's helping out. Only offer direction (and make it brief) when your child explicitly asks for it. Depending on the task, I find leaving the room to go do something else is quite a good idea (and, if you're anything like me, you can also apply this strategy when other grown-ups are loading the dishwasher or unpacking the shopping).

☐ Don't expect too much of your child, too quickly. This will rapidly make a sensitive child feel overwhelmed and hopeless – which leads, quite predictably, to apathy.

I feel I must mention, at this point – without wanting to cause a general despair in my audience – that our current societal setup and trends are not *at all* conducive towards happy collaboration in the home. Most of us grow up in nuclear or single-parent families, where one of the parents (as the main carer) is doing the lion's share of the housework, usually in a solitary state.

This situation isn't usually very good for that person's wellbeing, and the children see this. They are therefore – understandably – unlikely to feel motivated and joyful about joining in. Indeed, if the relationship with the parent is strong, they may end up, as older children, helping out purely out of an altruistic wish to not leave their parent all alone with it!

In situations of more communal living, there'd be more friends and family members around, working together in domestic settings much more happily and as equals. In such a scenario, I imagine kids would be more likely to help out *because they actively want to.*

I'm afraid there's not very much we can do about this, but I feel it would be unfair not to make a nod towards this reality – and just to recognize, out loud, why it's so hard for us to motivate our children towards helpful and joyful participation in our everyday living arrangements.

Respect, sensitivity, and gentleness

Neurodivergent children simply don't thrive in environments where there isn't a general sensitivity, respect, and kindness. In fact, they just can't deal with it! It may feel a little like 'tiptoeing around' at first, but in my view, we're all kinder and gentler with one another when there's someone present who just can't deal with us not being so. Just a few random tips about this, below:

☐ Don't walk in on your older child when they're in the bathroom or in their bedroom. Knock, or call out, and then wait for a positive answer, e.g. 'Yes, come in' (or equivalent), before entering.

☐ Try not to expose your child to disturbing films, images, or stories about people (in particular, animals and children) being severely hurt or badly treated.

☐ Be honest and open, however, about natural phenomena such as death and reproduction, should the topics come up.

☐ Do any pranks or jokes very gently indeed – testing the waters, so to speak. If people in your house don't like them, I'm afraid all that's going to need to be put on a back burner.

TO SUM UP

A 'family home' doesn't consist so much in its physical structure, but rather in the space that family happens to occupy. Of course, some spaces are way easier than others to adapt to a family's needs. The truth is that far too many people are obliged to live in situations that are not conducive to comfort and, in all too many cases, also do not offer much in terms of stability (e.g. involving financial insecurity and/or moving house a lot).

But if you manage, in the space you've got – even when it's against the odds – to create a safe, kind, and reassuring environment for your family (and this, of course, applies whatever your family's setup and constellation) – enough so that each person within it feels 'held' enough to be themselves, this is a great and wonderful achievement indeed.

whee -hee-hee!
— Gleefully glad
to be me!

CHAPTER 3

Downtime and Hobbies

Being absorbed in our own things, at our own pace. In these moments, all feels right with the world.

Neurodivergent children (and adults) need plenty of unstructured time to pursue our interests and hobbies. For us, this isn't a luxury to be enjoyed 'when all the work is done'. Instead, it's key to our mental, emotional, and physical wellbeing.

Some ideas on ways you can support your neurodivergent child in their downtime and hobbies are given below.

Stories, dramas, audiobooks, documentaries, and non-fiction

☐ Stories, novels, films, dramas, and series can be great for inspiration and relaxation. Follow your child's taste and preference, keeping in mind that they may watch the same show over and over, and/or still love things at ten that were meant for a five-year-old – and vice versa!

☐ Documentaries and fact books can be wonderful, too. Non-fiction is great for independent research and for developing a powerful imagination (although be careful about thinking it's fine to leave your kids in front of a nature documentary, only to find they've been totally traumatized on behalf of the baby caribou who didn't make it across the river).

☐ Download your child's favourite audiobooks. These are super handy as they can be listened to while doing other things, for example, when colouring, drawing, or in the bath.

☐ Comics are often a favourite with neurodivergent children, as they're often quite fantastical and so provide some wonderful downtime from 'real life'. In my experience, children can get really into copying the illustrations and even creating their own 'graphic novels'.

☐ Follow up on your *own* interests – by reading, listening to podcasts (or whatever your preferred medium), journalling, taking photos – just whatever you happen to be into!

When your kids see you regularly engaged, curious, and passionate about things, you're inadvertently showing-by-doing the concepts of motivation, meaning, and perseverance.

When I was writing the first draft of this book, my then seven-year-old daughter came to me to show me what she'd been up to all afternoon. It was a book she was writing, in a notebook. It was called, 'Dos and Don'ts for Baby Owls'.

Music

☐ Provide access to musical instruments, if possible. And there are some great apps for playing and producing music, too.

☐ Some musical experimenting, ideally in a relaxed and private environment, may reveal a strong interest in making and listening to music.[10]

☐ If your child/children enjoy listening to music, play some favourite tunes in the car (or for listening to on headphones when taking public transport) and make some family playlists trying to include everyone's preferences. We've had some great playlists alternating (for example) Beethoven, Madonna, The Clash, and the theme tunes to *Thomas the Tank Engine* and *Kipper the Dog*.

☐ When they're old enough, set your children up with what they need to make up and listen to their own playlists and albums.

☐ Try dancing together, as well. You may find your child/children love it – and you too, of course!

Animals and pets

Animals can have great therapeutic powers,[11] and the connection human-animal can be *especially* beneficial for neurodivergent children.[12]

☐ Organize time with animals and pets, if you can. Observe how your child gets on with them.

☐ If your life allows for its continued care, consider adopting a dog or cat, or even just a hamster, guinea pig or tortoise (I've heard there are some exceptionally intelligent and sociable species of tortoise – and they can be a great option for children who have allergies to animal hair).

☐ Some neurodivergent children become passionate about being with horses, and even about horse-riding, if they get the chance to do it (though note: they may be happiest in a non-competitive environment).

☐ If you're lucky, there may be places in your area designed for petting and meeting animals, some of which may offer this specifically for therapeutic purposes (on both sides!).[13]

☐ Just be aware pets have shorter lifespans than humans – this is especially true of some of the smaller ones such as guinea pigs and hamsters. See Chapter 11, 'Emotions', for information on processing loss and grief.

Special interests

For autistic and otherwise neurodivergent people, our special interests can often be quite central to our lives. Indeed, we often feel bereft if we don't have any projects on the go. Our dedication, passionate interest, and concentration (often to the exclusion of anything else) can be remarkable.[14]

On the positive side, this intensity can lead to great perseverance and even pinnacles of achievement (even if, at times, the world does not necessarily share our enthusiasm for a particular topic or project). On the downside, it can sometimes mean we might forget to do other things – even quite necessary things on occasion – like, for example, eating or sleeping. We may also feel sad when the project is over, in a similar way to a bereavement.

Overall, however, special interests are an amazing resource, as they brighten up our lives and give wonderful meaning to it all. Therefore, it's important to support your child in pursuing their interests as much as you can.

☐ From the beginning, observe closely what makes your child tick. When do their eyes light up, when do they look most alive? You could even take notes about it – when, where, what are we/they doing, who's here, what's the situation? (Personally, due to my unreliable short-term memory, I often take notes. Indeed, that's where this book came from. And yes, before you ask, figuring out what works for my child *did* become one of my biggest special interests!)

☐ Once you're getting an idea of what they're into, you can support your child's interests – perhaps involving things like building, science, music, art, or looking after animals and plants. Try to ensure there's enough time and resources, and suitable space, to allocate to these hobbies.

☐ See if you can locate mentors, or even (in some cases, i.e. only when appropriate and desired by your child) workshops, groups, or teachers for your child. More on this in Chapter 7, 'Learning and School'.

☐ Roll with it. Even if you (and/or the world) have no clue why this particular human being feels so intensely compelled to pursue these particular interests, there will be a reason. Somewhere.

> The special interest is unlikely to be predictable and can even be difficult to spot. I've heard neurodivergent people saying they feel left out as they don't have a 'special interest'. Then it transpires that they have intimate knowledge of every item and block in Minecraft (and what you can do with it), or have a stack of beautiful home-made rag rugs in the cupboard and a collection of fabric that would put any charity shop to shame, or they know every part of a bicycle and what it does, or they can name every football player who's scored for Germany in the last 30 years.

☐ When getting presents for your child, get them something they want or have asked for, rather than being inadvertently influenced by your views on what you think they *should* want or need.

☐ Be prepared, especially for those with ADHD, that special interests may disappear overnight, and be replaced (perhaps immediately, perhaps after a time) with other ones. Some hobbies may lie dormant and be picked up later, and others may just disappear into the mists of time. This is normal. Again, as a parent, patience (resignation?) may be required – especially if you've invested in something. But whatever you do, try *very* hard not to put any pressure on your child, as this will only make them feel guilty, and can quickly lead to shame, low self-esteem, and emotional withdrawal.

☐ Be aware that we neurodivergent people may often use our special interests to de-stress and calm ourselves down.

Special interests to de-stress – and when they may become obsessive

The intensity of our interest in things may fluctuate alongside our emotional state. The nature of special interests, in my experience, is that they can be rather a two-edged sword.

While, for example, learning Mandarin might be a useful skill for me one day (who knows) I'm also aware I'm using the language app to regulate my emotional state. On a day when I'm having trouble coping, I may earn a few hundred points! The truth is, it calms me. A lot. This is because I find it a much simpler and more linear world than 'out there'.

So perhaps – instead of honing my language skills to the point where I could, theoretically at least, chair at international conferences – I may also want to look at what's happening in my life and why I feel such a strong need to go into my own world *quite* so much.

Sorry, back to the children! So, if your child's special interest looks like it's becoming all-consuming:

☐ Don't just veto the interest (recipe for disaster!).
☐ Instead, try to focus on a) reducing your child's anxiety levels

overall, and b) doing some other fun things together that you both/all enjoy (more on this in Chapter 4, 'Out and About').

☐ Be aware that the relaxing influence of a special interest can be used to advantage. I know one child who, after any social interaction (even if it was fun), needs to walk around the car park comparing all the makes, models, and maximum speeds, for just as long as it takes to regain his inner equilibrium.

Screentime

This topic is enormous for most families these days, as our use of screens and the internet has so heavily influenced the landscape of socializing, recreation, and education.

In some regards, for example, for Augmentative and Alternative Communication (AAC) or social networking (facilitating, among other things, the advent of a global and vibrant autistic/neurodivergent community) the advantages are enormous.

That said, it doesn't come without its problems and challenges.

While the technologies have often become (for both children and their families) a lifeline, there's no harm in a) being equipped with knowledge about the effects of being on screens for lengths of time (perhaps especially for those with hypersensitivities),[15] and b) having some strategies up our sleeves for achieving, or regaining, some balance around it when necessary.

Some positives and negatives of screens, for kids

Positives:

- For children who don't communicate through speaking, the technology, if they have access to it, is a game-changer.
- For everyone, it offers some downtime (but most especially, I think, for exhausted and overwhelmed parents).

- Being on a screen is a lot of fun – in so many ways!
- It can be very educational, both in terms of the material available, and the technology itself – especially if you can get a laptop or desktop computer (i.e. it's not just usable for gaming or being online, but they'll learn lots of technical skills as well).
- For older children it's great for having a social life and friends online. They may, just like us adults, 'find their tribe' this way.
- It provides an opportunity to become good at something and, through that, gain valuable self-confidence.

Negatives:

- It takes time away from other pursuits. This can, if it becomes regular and time-consuming, also lead to unfitness (as being on a screen doesn't usually involve moving about very much).
- Too much screentime can exacerbate, and even cause, difficulty concentrating and shortened attention span.[16]
- It can cause sleeping problems in children. [17]
- Over time, excessive use of screens can contribute to conditions such as depression, obesity, and even (in some cases) anxiety.[18]
- It can also give rise to a huge and terrible boredom[19] when doing anything besides being on the screen. This is due to its addictive nature.[20]

The highly addictive nature of screens is not so much in the technology itself as constructed by its algorithms.

If the motivation behind providing online content to the public were not profit, then the algorithms used could observe what patterns of use best complement people's lives and habits in terms of our wellbeing (physical and emotional) and then optimize the content, and the ways it's presented, towards that aim.

Currently, however, the algorithms' main aims are a) getting us to engage more within the online context/platform, and b) showing us more adverts (and alongside these, gathering vast amounts of data on whatever will make us do those two things the most). It's pretty basic. Indeed, it's a bit embarrassing, societally speaking – I mean, if we had to explain this to the aliens.

So, whether it's about gaming, social media, or just watching YouTube shorts or scrolling through posts on Instagram or TikTok – it's the algorithms that are the biggest driver behind the extremely addictive nature of being on a device.

Obviously, there are many and varied ways a screen may be being used – some of which have more, and some fewer, of the effects listed above. It's a vast, nuanced, and complex subject! And one where we parents have the added disadvantage that our children (once past the age of about six) are often way more tech-savvy than we are.

Below are some tips that may help us, as parents, to keep at least a little bit of the contents of Pandora's box from escaping – too quickly anyway – into the wild. But please, be very forgiving of yourself here. Only do what feels possible and right for your family. This is very tricky stuff! When it comes to screens and connectivity, I picture us parents as tiny, rather confused, superhero figurines standing in front of a huge and rapidly descending avalanche of the unknown. I hope this may give a visual impression of why it might feel a little *hard* sometimes.

☐ If it's humanly (and humanely) possible, keep your child, especially when they're very young, from having too much screentime (excepting devices used for AAC). How? Hm, yes. More in the following tips.

☐ Limit the time you spend on your own device when you're with your children. Switch off notifications and resist the urge to check your phone. Find a time to do your social media, check your emails and so on, at times when your children aren't with you.

☐ Have other pastimes available for sit-down moments with your kids, both at home and in your bag for when you're out and about. For small children, maybe colouring books and crayons, feely-books. For slightly older ones, comic books, drawing pads, coloured pencils, box-puzzles.

☐ On journeys, audiobooks and music can be great as an alternative to screens, as the children can look out of the window and daydream.

☐ Play some games together in moments when there's not much to do. Charades. The 'don't walk on the cracks' game if you're on a pavement. Or the 'what colour is the next car going to be' game, or 'guess how many buses will go by before our one arrives'.

But if you're rapidly losing the will to live just reading this, please hand your child your smartphone. Your mental health is of greater importance than keeping your children from being on a screen. While all of what I'm saying here is 'the high ideal', I know only too well how exhausting it can all be, and how sometimes if we don't get those five minutes of downtime ourselves (right now!), things could go... well, horribly wrong.

☐ Show curious and impartial interest, if your children do spend time online, in what they spend the time doing. 'Hey, so in this "Minecraft", are you really mining for something?' and so on. If they're anything like my kids they'll really enjoy enlightening you. This paves the way for them being happy to tell you, both now and later, quite a lot about their 'inner world'.

☐ If your (slightly older) child has a gaming setup, consider keeping it outside of their bedroom, at least until they hit their teens.

Perhaps a dedicated area in the corner of your living room, or on a wide landing, or in an office space. 'Sleeping headspace', I find, is very different from 'gaming headspace' (similarly to how, for us adults, it's preferable to keep our 'office space' separate from our bedroom).

☐ If the 'fight with the screen' is getting you down, but you want to persevere, you could arrange a holiday (or every now and then, a weekend away) with no electronic devices. Some types of holidays naturally lend themselves to this, like a campervan or camping, or a wooden cabin in the Alps (oops, some fantasy crept in there!).

☐ Tell your child openly and neutrally about the addictive nature of screens – perhaps focusing on your own experience. I think it's not so bad if they see how you may struggle with it too.

☐ Don't use 'screentime', or time playing their favourite game/s, to reward a child for doing something else you want them to do. I'd also advise against using this feature in any 'parental control' apps you may use for regulating screentime.

One interesting effect of rewarding someone for doing something is that whatever you have to do to get the reward becomes less and less attractive, while whatever the reward consists of becomes more and more attractive. This is a basic feature of human psychology that I feel gets rather overlooked, for example, in our education system.[21]

Things you'd rather your child didn't see

☐ Don't act shocked by anything you might uncover, or that your child reveals to you, about their time online.

☐ Preferably when your child is still a toddler, set up firewalls against adult content on all your devices (either using 'parental controls' on the device itself, or in your account settings with your provider).

☐ If you have a kid who's into gaming and/or has same-aged or older friends, accept that sooner or later they *will* be exposed to pornography and/or other disturbing material – yes, even if they don't actively seek it out. And probably far younger than you ever thought possible.

If your child is exposed to pornography and comes to you about it (or you suspect it, in which case you'll need to approach the topic terribly, terribly gently and as a very general concept), understand that, being extremely sensitive (and the majority of porn not generally focusing on the beauties of mutual physical love and connection) they'll probably already be in agonies of shame and confusion.

It can be worth saying to your child that, if they feel/felt pulled in, all it shows is that they're 100 per cent human. And it's absolutely not their fault these things exist and are put in front of us.

It may feel worth mentioning to your child, as well, that the human sentiments around sex and intimacy that pull us into it are actually all about mutual love, connection, and emotional fulfilment. Beautiful stuff. And the only reason commercial pornography isn't so much is because it happens to be profit-driven (i.e. it wants you to be addicted to *porn*, not to human connection!) and that's why it morphs into 'extreme' before you can say 'boo'.[22]

There's some great literature about love and sex available these days for children and young people – as well as documentaries, TV programmes, and so on – that show love, connection, and some physical intimacy (though obviously you'll need to keep a careful eye on what is age-appropriate for your child).[23] It's tricky, but I think it's by far the best for children to already have a reasonable awareness about the topic – in a loving, caring, connected, and emotionally healthy context – *before* they start coming across material online.

What about rules?

If you decide to have rules in your house around screentime, you'll need to a) feel able to be firm and organized enough to apply those rules (if you're feeling overwhelmed by your life overall, it may not be the right moment), b) have a strong enough connection with your child, at the time, for it not to impact your relationship negatively, and c) be aware that children may well be using their device for comfort/familiarity (as a kind of security blanket). If this is the case, you'll need to provide alternative emotional safety nets for them if reducing its use. More on how to do this in Chapter 11, 'Emotions' and Chapter 12, 'Bedtime'.

If these conditions are in place, the following tips contain suggestions on some ways screentime could be regulated.

☐ Maybe allow TV only in the evening, and even then perhaps, a) not right before bed, and b) only films, series, or documentaries (i.e. best to avoid flicking about watching short videos and adverts on TikTok or YouTube).

☐ Maybe dedicate an evening or two to watching films, dramas, documentaries (or whatever fits your and your children's taste) together.

☐ You could stick to not using screens in the car (audiobooks or music only).

☐ You could put in place strategies for limiting screentime. Here are some ways to do this:

To allow screentime only for certain times of day and/or for certain purposes, some options are:

- Hold the codes to your children's devices.
- Put devices away in a drawer or lockbox, to bring out at certain times (note: this should never be used either to reward or punish children).
- Install a 'parental control' app on devices to monitor and limit your child's screentime. There are many available, also free ones.
- Use 'Access Controls' to place time restrictions on WiFi access in your home, or on specific devices. This can be done online through your account with your internet provider.

If you do limit screentime, you'll need to make sure your child has access to all the company and reassurance they need (this is especially important at night, for example, for children who have trouble sleeping) because if you've allowed online access up until now, they may be using their device for companionship and distraction.

If applying restrictions is causing problems in your home it may be best to ease up on the rules, at least temporarily, and turn your attention instead to doing enjoyable things together and strengthening your connection (more on this in Chapter 6, 'Communication' and Chapter 5, 'Friendship') before any renewed attempt. One good option can be a holiday or weekend away together without devices.

Our hobbies, and what they mean to us

Your child's engagement and 'spark' – around their special interests, pastimes, and hobbies – can be an external indictor for their wellbeing overall, which gives this chapter perhaps unexpected importance in the scheme of things.

If you're not seeing any signs of enthusiasm in your child at the moment, and instead are seeing apathy or emotional withdrawal:

☐ Look for ways to increase feelings of safety and self-esteem (more in Chapter 1, 'Basics'; Chapter 2, 'At Home'; Chapter 5, 'Friendship'; and Chapter 6, 'Communication').

☐ Promote autonomy and motivation through helping them to feel more in control of their lives (see this chapter; Chapter 4, 'Out and About'; Chapter 7, 'Learning and School'; and Chapter 11, 'Emotions').

☐ Look for ways to improve physical health and comfort (see Chapter 2, 'At Home' and Chapter 9, 'Health, Hygiene, and Fitness').

TO SUM UP

Each family is unique, and each person's situation is going to be different in regard to their preferred hobbies and the activities that hold meaning for them. Notwithstanding this, there are some universals – such as finding the time and being relaxed enough to indulge our interests and having the basic materials with which to do so. And this is something I'd wish for everyone – both for ourselves, and for our children!

What's outside my door today, d'you think?

CHAPTER 4
Out and About

The most wonderful adventures await us, out there in the world.

Being out and about can be fun, stimulating, and great for learning. Seeing that life out there can be wonderful (if a little unpredictable sometimes) is important for any child, but it becomes especially so for those susceptible to overwhelm.

If we get it right, we pave the way for great things – confidence and positivity among them. But, as most of us know only too well, being out and about with our neurodivergent children can go both ways. It can be either wonderful and magical, or a complete nightmare (for them and us)!

In the next pages there are lots of practical tips that I hope may help to bring about *more* of the former and *less* of the latter.

- ☐ Take things slowly and gently, living as much in the moment as you can.
- ☐ Check there's access to somewhere reasonably quiet and private

on demand. It's easier for car owners, but other options could be public gardens or parks, picnic areas, libraries, community centres, or child-friendly (and not too busy) cafes.

☐ Don't bank on your child's participation, for example, at social events. Bring along their ear-defenders, some comics, a colouring book, a talking book, or a model or puzzle they can do – or, of course, an electronic device (though note: bringing along a device can be rather a mixed blessing as, if you feel your child might actually enjoy taking part in any of the activities or games or socializing on any level, it can be extremely difficult – not to mention conflictual – to try to get them to put the device to the side for a bit in order to try other things out).

☐ Spend regular time outdoors, doing non-competitive, non-structured activities. Examples could be: playing in a sandpit or playpark, tree climbing (low ones if your child isn't very confident), paddling (lake, river, beach, if you have any of those available to you), walks and scrambles – and even, for older and more actively inclined kids, things like swimming, sledging, horse-riding, or fishing.

Neurodivergent people regularly become overwhelmed by social dynamics and 'other people' in general (especially in any competitive context and/or where there's any pressure or expectation). Additional triggers can be noise, artificial lighting, feeling trapped and unable to escape, and feeling pressure or hurried along, for example, in queues or busy places overall.

These elements are usually absent in natural environments such as the countryside or, failing that, parks and gardens, or open public spaces (anywhere there's no traffic). It's also nice to be in places where people won't judge (or even notice!) children who make noise, run, jump about, and so on. We used to spend quite a lot of time in a disused carpark near to our home, with the kids' trikes or scooters, and the dog.

☐ Find some good playparks. These would ideally have lots of space, some greenery, and few people (or go at times when they're quiet). Swings, see-saws, roundabouts, climbing frames, slides, and trampolines can be great fun and good exercise too. You may see your child revelling in certain types of movement – for example, spinning around or swinging.

☐ When you go on outings, take lots of time to meander and explore, and observe your surroundings. Avoid hurrying and being goal oriented (the more time your child spends 'in the moment', the better!).

☐ Don't make people pose for pictures if they're unwilling, nor take any pictures or videos of your children unless they're completely happy with it (and if you take any they don't like, delete them without protest). Note: if you do this consistently, your child will have less of an issue with having their photo taken than if they aren't consulted.

☐ For holidays or weekends, perhaps visit somewhere quiet and unpressured, and/or in nature, if possible – for example, woods, lake, seaside. It can make a really refreshing change. If there are certain places (or one place) that become your favourites and to which you return regularly, then so much the better.

☐ Give a good few minutes' warning before changing setting for example, leaving the house, leaving a playground, the beach. Make sure you get an answer confirming they got the message (if they're concentrating on something else, they may not have heard a word you said).

☐ If your kid loses something (for example when trying to leave the house and everyone's already sitting in the car), just quietly and calmly help them look for it. In moments like this, if a big fuss is made and *especially* if they're the focus, a neurodivergent child's anxiety can go through the roof.

Commitments, errands, and engagements

☐ Try to be prepared beforehand – for example, by bringing along some drinks, snacks, and activities (later, you might be very thankful you did so).

☐ If going anywhere public (e.g. public transport), make sure you bring along your sunflower lanyard, if you have one. Wearing this (whether for yourself and/or your child) helps others make accommodations for you. Plus, overall, it just means everyone will be kinder.

☐ Aim to arrive early to appointments. Leaving more time means you'll be less stressed when setting out, and the journey will be pleasanter (and possibly less dangerous) than otherwise.

☐ Wherever possible, avoid running errands with your child when you're tired and stressed yourself, or in a rush.

☐ Again wherever possible, try to allow lots of time for errands, leaving chunks of time between commitments, for example, leaving the house and catching a train. For instance, I find it's much better to be playing a 'spot the train' game for 20 minutes, than to be rushing.

☐ Try to not have too many time-constrained appointments. I think one a day is quite enough, and at least a couple of days a week it's good to have none at all.

☐ If at all possible, avoid places where overstimulation is likely, for example, shopping malls, supermarkets, and any other crowded, noisy places with artificial lights and little natural green or sky.

☐ See if it's possible to do your shopping and other errands at times when few people are around, even if that means changing your routines.

☐ Try to be relaxed, take time, and involve your child – they could find items on the list, push the trolley, choose the fruit, and so on.

Avoiding over-stimulation

☐ Carry a set of noise-cancelling headphones in case of unavoidable noisy situations.

☐ Have a pair of sunglasses handy for your child to wear if they find it too bright.

☐ Learn to recognize the signs of over-stimulation. Distress signals (though you know your own child best) could be anything from high-pitched noises to repetitive movements or tics. If this happens, change environment as quickly and calmly as possible (I know, I don't really need to tell you this).

☐ Avoid eating in crowded or noisy restaurants or cafes, or very formal ones where you must 'behave'. Maybe bring (or buy) a picnic instead, so you can eat somewhere quieter and more private.

Outings and getting around

☐ If your toddler hates being belted in, with highchairs and prams/strollers it's usually possible to find ways around having to firmly strap your child in (more on this below).

☐ Whenever you can (i.e. perhaps not in the middle of rush hour on a busy road) give your child the option of either sitting in the pram/stroller or not, as they wish. Small children might, for example, really enjoy pushing it together with you instead, standing in the circle of your arms. And if your child has some autonomy over climbing in and out (when the situation allows – i.e. on bumpy surfaces the straps might be necessary to hold your child safely in), they'll be much happier during outings. Note: If your child is prone to leaping out suddenly, without much warning, try letting them know – perhaps humorously – that while it's fine to do it, it really is best if they give you a shout, or a signal, when they're about to alight!

☐ When it comes to their car seat, try giving your child as much autonomy as you can, as early as it's feasible. The more they feel in control – climbing in, pulling their own seatbelt on and clipping it in – the happier they'll be with the whole idea.

☐ In the car, try to give your child some control and joint ownership over the environment for example, they could open and close their own window, choose the music, and so on. For us, picnic boxes also helped a lot – I'd strategically combine belting the children in with handing them their little picnic boxes (nothing very exciting, but there is just *something* about food in boxes!).

☐ Games such as a simple puzzle or cards (maybe not ones with lots of small pieces), or even just guessing games such as 'I spy', are great for passing the time on a train or bus.

> I'm just remembering, when the children were little, us getting on the train into town (a 45-minute journey) and me saying, having forgotten on this occasion to put any games or cards in my bag, 'Hey, let's play the story-telling game' (each of us would say one word, through this making up a story, for example if you say 'Once', I might say, 'upon'). I started. 'The', I said, then turned to my son expectantly. 'End', he said. The train hadn't even started moving.

☐ Don't feel there's always a need to prepare things within an inch of their lives, especially when going on pleasant outings.

☐ Try not to panic if you've forgotten things. Instead, see if you can cheerfully make do with what you have. A parent who always carries everything one could possibly need could make for children who get fixed to the notion that you *must* have those things to be okay, and that it's a crisis if you don't.

☐ Make spontaneous decisions together about doing fun things. Hey, why don't we go to the beach or lake? Yes, even with no towels or swimming things (if you happen to already be out)! Just make sure everyone's on board with what's happening.

☐ But don't push kids out of their comfort zone through persuasion. If (say, in the example I've given above) your child prefers to snuggle in a blanket while the others wade in the water or dig in the sand, that's perfect too. Maybe spend a bit of time snuggling with them, if they want that, or sitting/playing close to them – or you could even try to find something they do want to do that makes them more included, but without pushing them into anything they're reluctant to do.

Often, with a little imagination, it's not either/or. It's nice to feel included, and cared about, even when you don't feel very outgoing. And it can really help a child who's feeling less sociable or adventurous to have another human present who's not doing the whole 'group' thing either.

☐ Bring your book or a magazine on outings – or sometimes go with a good friend, if possible – so you can sit down and enjoy the minutes you get while your children explore and play, wherever they wish to stop for a bit (provided it's not the lion's pen at the zoo).

☐ Make intentional stops in places where there's enough space to play, perhaps in nature with no structured activities, though playparks are great too.

☐ Try to remember to bring a flask of coffee or tea along for the grown-up/s, or, if the place permits, get yourself a nice takeaway latte (or whatever your preference!).

☐ Avoid pressurizing your child into doing activities against their will – though note, this doesn't preclude some negotiation! Just make sure they're comfortable and on board if agreeing to something that isn't their favourite choice. You could say, for example, 'How about we try it and, if you don't like it after 15 minutes, we can leave?' (But you *must* be true to your promise and flexible too if, for example, after five minutes you can see they can't bear a moment longer!)

☐ As gracefully as you can manage, let your child back out of things they said they'd do, or previously expressed a wish to do, but they've now changed their mind about. They may have not properly understood or known what it entailed.

It may seem rather counter-intuitive at first, but real self-discipline, perseverance, and motivation come from inside a person, and (unfortunately) not from having things imposed on them by others. No matter how frustrating it may be for others (such as parents) to endure the process while biting our tongues.[24]

☐ Try not to use the phrase, 'be careful', as this can trigger feelings of fear and helplessness in the face of some unspecified danger. Instead, give specific warnings and only when necessary. Try to frame them as observations, for example, 'This is a very busy road' or 'These branches are very spiky.'

Meltdown

It can happen that your child becomes overwhelmed and/or that some unforeseen thing happens that tips the balance and sends your child into meltdown.

Sometimes, there's simply no way for a parent to predict or avoid a meltdown situation. Here you are – with your child on the brink of a meltdown or already in the middle of one. Your heart has sunk into your boots. It's a nightmare situation. Especially if it's happening in public, and/or if you've other kids to take care of, and/or it's in a place that's loud and busy and there's no getting away from easily (I'm shuddering while I write).

In this section you'll find tips on what to do before (if you spot it coming in time), during, and after a meltdown.

But first, let's look at what it feels like from the perspective of the person having the meltdown. Here are some descriptions:

'Bad emotion – usually self-loathing, but shame works, too – grows and becomes everything, obliterating my sense of self. I become pain. Then I hurt myself because I'm desperate to get the bad feelings out.'

'Like you're going to explode. I usually end up hitting and biting myself. And ripping my hair out when trying to resist head banging. Pulling my ears. Ripping my clothes. It feels like intense frustration and then hopelessness.'

'Everything is ten times louder, brighter, even existing is stressful. It is often impossible to think. You lose control of your body. Everyone else is suddenly speaking a foreign language that you don't know, and it sounds like they're yelling at you ('cause everything's louder now). Friends and family may look like strangers – why are these strangers touching and yelling at me??? Stop it!!'

Yup, so that's what it feels like. At this point we may realize we're quite lucky to not be the ones actually having the meltdown (or else, perhaps we rather wish we were, if it meant our child would not have to go through it). So – now let's look at what to *do* about it!

Let's return to our own perspective as parents – perhaps by now feeling a bit like the Hobbits facing the climb up Mount Doom.

Why the meltdown?

Figuring out the reasons for meltdowns and the patterns behind them is essential, as there may be ways to pre-empt them – and, at times, avoid them happening altogether.

Meltdowns are generally accumulative – in other words a

meltdown has been 'simmering' for a while – so the person has been feeling overall anxious, stressed, and 'on the edge' for a protracted length of time. That said, there are always going to be specific reasons for a meltdown to happen *when* it does. The following is a list of things to make note of in any meltdown scenario.

If the meltdown happened apparently spontaneously, or 'out of nowhere':

- sensory overwhelm: bright lights, loud noises, lots of people, small spaces (perhaps feeling trapped and/or claustrophobic)
- tiredness, hunger and/or too hot or cold
- an undercurrent of feeling from others or the environment – such as stress and/or censure and/or a general sense of hurry or pressure – or an expectation you're unequipped to fulfil
- a change might have happened too suddenly – particularly if it's an unpleasant one (we neurodivergent people can have a *lot* of trouble with changes of focus – and *especially* ones we're not in control of)[25]
- shock, sadness, and/or powerlessness about things we're witnessing or have witnessed. I have a friend who, as a child, melted down in the zoo after seeing the orangutans ('they looked so... sad!')
- a trigger (perhaps a sound, smell, or person) that's brought up some painful memory or past experience, often on a subconscious level.[26]

If the meltdown happened as a result of someone requiring or requesting something from the child, or vetoing something:

- Again, maybe the child is simply overwhelmed and upset (see the above points). Perhaps something has become a 'designated issue' – after all, it's far more manageable to for example, express that you'll die if you don't get a chocolate ice cream, than to consciously realize your senses have just been overwhelmed, you've disappointed people you care about, or that you were witness to something you couldn't emotionally deal with.

- Another thing to consider though, when it comes to a child frequently and vocally focusing on strong, specific (and bite-sized) demands, is that they may *often* feel little or no control over what's happening, both from moment to moment and in their lives overall. And/or they might *often* feel not listened to or not taken seriously. And/or they may *often* feel they're put into situations they can't cope with or where they feel powerless or defenceless.

Action stations

And finally, we come to what a parent can do for their child when a meltdown occurs.

- ☐ Try to drop into 'calm mode'. Take a second to imagine how your child may be feeling right now. Your compassion, when you do this, might replace any (very natural!) feelings of frustration, embarrassment, or overwhelm yourself.
- ☐ Stand – or sit or kneel, depending on the situation – between your child and any other people, or else (if your child is allowing you to hold them) position yourself with the child facing away from any groups or crowds, or with your body shielding them.
- ☐ Don't be tempted to ask, 'what's wrong?' People experiencing strong emotions usually can't answer that question.
- ☐ Speak in a low, reassuring tone. You can stick to a mantra-like phrase such as 'I'm here love, I'm here' or even just 'Mm, mm'.
- ☐ Don't focus your direct gaze or attention onto someone who's having a meltdown. Focused attention can feel painful, even

threatening, to a person who's showing strong feelings they have no control over.

☐ If you think excessive/inescapable noise may have triggered the meltdown (e.g. if your child's making high-pitched noises/ screams and/or clamping their hands over their ears), and if it's impossible to either move them or make the noise go away, offer your child their noise-cancelling headphones.

☐ Offer your child any preferred comforting items, toys, or teddies – perhaps simply by laying them within reach if your child doesn't want you too close.

☐ Allow them to stim freely ('stimming' is any repetitive motion or behaviour whose purpose is to emotionally self-regulate), offering them whatever they need to do so. (Note: if the stim is a self-harmful one, such as hitting themselves or banging their head against something, tips on what to do about this can be found in the section on 'Stimming' in Chapter 11, 'Emotions'.)

☐ Bear in mind that, if you were the person with your child and relating to them when the meltdown occurred, you may have inadvertently had a hand in causing it. That means that your child's emotional explosion may be directed, at least partially, at you. Not to mention that you may be feeling pretty ropey, right now, as well!

☐ So – considering the above – do everything you can to show your child it's *truly* okay to express their emotions and that you take their feelings to be valid. More ways on how to help your child express anger effectively but without harming themselves or others are given in Chapter 11, 'Emotions', in the section on 'Anger'.

☐ When and if your child is amenable to you being close to them, get as close as you can to them, preferably at their level so perhaps kneeling or sitting (depending on the situation), but without physically imposing. Speak in a low tone, again reassuring them, calmly and gently, that you are there when they need you.

The idea is to be available for hugs, reassurance, and holding, but *only if and when they want it.*

☐ The presence of an animal can help diffuse a meltdown. Indeed, there are some animals – usually dogs – who've been trained to do so.[27]

☐ Only if/when this is possible without any physical forcing or restraint, try to guide your child somewhere more comfortable, private, and with lower sensory input (not as bright, noisy, busy, etc.).

What about 'tantrums'?

This is what we might call a meltdown that we view as being voluntary (i.e. it's our perception that the child should have some control over themselves). This tends to happen as the result of something unwanted happening, or because of a carer vetoing a request (which is, I think, why we may see it as voluntary on the part of the child).

☐ Don't apply any blame or judgement and try not to be angry or impatient with the child.

☐ If the meltdown was triggered by vetoing something, bear in mind there are invariably larger issues at play. Make a pact with yourself to look more closely at what these things may be when you next get the chance. (More information on what these 'larger issues' may be, and how to deal with them, can be found in Chapter 11, 'Emotions'.)

☐ There are times when it's best (depending on the situation) to simply humour a child, postponing thinking about bigger issues, and what to do about them, to a more convenient moment.

☐ If, however, your child's demand is impossible, too expensive and/or too inconvenient, calmly make it clear to them that it can't be fulfilled – not like this, at least. Give a reason (or the reasons) – the simpler and the more truthful the better.

☐ If you're being irresistibly drawn into an argument, say that you're willing to discuss it later (*discuss*, not necessarily *fulfil!*), in a different and less stressful situation. Even suggest a specific time and place where you'll discuss it with them, and then make *certain* you come through on this. Don't leave it to them to press the issue, as they'll stop believing you when you say this.

☐ In an 'unreasonable demand' situation, at times it can help to offer a child things 'in fantasy'. For example, if they don't just want one giant lollipop but two, or three, you could say, 'Hey, imagine if we could have the whole shopful – or even the whole factory! We'd have a pile as tall as this building!'[28]

☐ Another thing that can help, in some situations, is taking a few photos of the desired item/s.

There will be times when the thing your child is asking for in the moment is truly, deeply, genuinely important to them. If they still want the same thing tomorrow and the next day – and the week after, and the week after that – then it might be time to start considering what can be done towards fulfilling that particular wish. And of course, the more trust your child has that you *will* help them in fulfilling things that are of genuine importance to them, the less frequently this type of meltdown will occur.

When things are getting calmer
Once things are calming down a bit, you can look for more ways to assist your child depending on the situation, on knowing them, and on what you're seeing/sensing in them right now.

☐ Check if your child wants to be held or wants a hug. Make sure they know that's available as soon as they want it.

☐ See if they're too cold or too hot. If you think they're cold, offer a blanket or scarf; if you think they're too hot, try gently removing any coats or jumpers.

☐ Check if they're hungry or thirsty, and if so, offer them a drink or a cereal bar, fruit, or other snack.

☐ Sometimes, depending on the situation, providing your child with their favourite music, or putting on one of their talking books, can help – the familiar sounds and voices can be calming.

☐ Tentatively offer your child any favourite toys or stims (spinners, feelies for texture), if you have those with you. I have a friend whose child adores the texture of her fluffy scarf, so she would offer her that. If there's a risk things might get thrown, perhaps choose soft objects to start with.

☐ If they find your voice soothing, perhaps talk about passing things they might be interested in, or tell a story, using a sort of 'narrative' tone where there's clearly no obligation to listen to the content, nor reply.

☐ Try counting aloud, either objects or just sequentially. This one's nice as your child may join in if they're starting to feel a bit better.

☐ Try, after a meltdown, to stick to offering things that are *healing* and not just *distracting*.

Anaesthetizing emotional pain

When we hand an upset child a lollipop or a smartphone, we're basically giving them an introductory course on emotional numbing. This risks forming associations that can lead to addictive behaviour. My sister gently pointed this out to me when I gave my son chocolate straightaway when he bumped his knee. He was about three, if I remember. Though it worked beautifully in the moment, I did – with some horror, actually – understand what she meant and take it on board.

☐ If nothing's working, and there's no other responsible adult present, try to fall into a meditative space. See if you can remember a specific time or memory when things were loving and harmonious with your child. Try to imagine it, with all the details – their face, their smile, *and* those feelings of wonderful closeness and love you were feeling (this child in front of you is, believe it or not, the same one).

☐ Stay quiet, unobtrusive, and present, *if* that's possible, in other words, unless you feel like something bad might happen if you do – in which case, if the situation allows, go into another room leaving the door open. And wait it out.

☐ It's important, tempting as it is, not to blame ourselves here (jumping onto the 'blame the parents' bandwagon).[29] For a start, we're *really* doing our best, and also (more practically) shame naturally triggers either apathy and helplessness, or a self-protect (defence) response in us. Self-compassion, on the other hand, brings about self-awareness and is enabling.

The aftermath

☐ After a meltdown, your child might feel drained and very tired. If this happens when you're out and you can't get them home (and don't have a private vehicle available), tuck them into their pram, if they'll accept that, or carry them in your arms.

☐ In all scenarios stay with, or failing that, near your child. If you're at home or at a friend's or family member's house, sit or lie with them for as long as they need it.

☐ And throughout all this – try to convey through your bearing, body language, and actions that you love and accept them unconditionally, and that this is not a hassle for you. Their wellbeing is top priority right now.

HOW TO RAISE HAPPY NEUROFABULOUS CHILDREN

Some reflection

☐ It's very tempting, once a meltdown is over, to wipe the whole episode from your memory. However, it's incredibly useful to reflect and even take notes. What happened beforehand? Where were you? What was noticeable about the surrounding environment? Who were you with? And so on.

☐ Depending on your child, they *might* want to talk with you about it all – but let them take the lead on this. If they want to try to collaboratively a) figure things out, and b) find ways to make things easier in the future – then wow, fantastic! But don't ever put pressure on your child to talk things over. More on this in Chapter 11, 'Emotions'.

☐ And finally, don't forget that episodes like this leave emotional bruises on both you and your child. So, plan for some healing time and pleasant activities, both alone (if possible, as you'll need nurturing too), and together with your child, to renew and strengthen your connection.

☐ To give some perspective, I think meltdowns happen in pretty much *all* families. Life rarely allows us to avoid them completely. So just remember – they do pass.

TO SUM UP

And here we come to the end of the 'Out and About' chapter. Besides the part about meltdowns, I'm aware a lot of this chapter has been about relaxing, enjoying life, taking time, and taking things as they come. But I'm also aware that if your life is stressful, hurried, quite isolated, and full of multi-tasking – as so many parents' lives are – how that could all look like pie-in-the-sky. Parents, in our society, are very alone in our struggles – and often quite poor, too. It would be great if lots of assistance and a vibrant community were on our doorstep, but let's face it, they usually are not.

So, if you've read about things you'd love to try out theoretically, but you know that taking on more or introducing any changes is going to mean additional stress or work for you, please go *very* easy on yourself. Only do what feels fully doable – and if it's causing stress, stop! As parents, our own physical, emotional, and mental health is fundamental to the whole enterprise.

CHAPTER 5

Friendship

Feeling understood by others, and enjoying their companion-ship, is food for the soul.

When we think of friendships among children, we may picture groups of same-aged children hanging out in playparks or in the school yard. With your neurodivergent child this is unlikely to be the scene. And, as much as our cultural bias may tell us otherwise, this is actually not a bad thing! Your child's greatest friendships and connections in their lives may well turn out to be unexpected ones.

To start with, neurodivergent people need certain conditions to be in place before we can make meaningful connections with other people. Here are some of them (this will vary from person to person, so I've only put those which seem to be common to most neurodivergent people):

- a non-stressful environment
- no feelings of pressure/expectation

- no feelings of shame or inadequacy
- not feeling that being yourself is just *not* going to work here
- feeling free to talk about what you're interested in
- feeling free to wander off, or appear distracted, without offending anyone
- enough time and opportunities to have both on-time and off-time when others are about
- something else to focus on that's not each other (awkward!)
- not feeling pressure to talk/chat
- someone present who notices when you are unable to socialize for a moment longer (it could be the 'rabbit-in-the-headlights' look…or else you're stimming like anything, or you've started bouncing off the walls, or…okay, there could be different signs).

Here are some tips on ways we can help our neurodivergent children make meaningful connections with other people.

☐ Seek out and spend time with people you know love your child and who see their good qualities.

☐ Nurture connections with people who see your child as an interesting and special person, and who feel some connection with them, maybe due to similar interests (there's more on how to do this in the section 'Making friends' below).

☐ Bear in mind a lot of autistic children prefer older (or younger) people to kids their age, and friendships don't have to remain in any specific age group.

☐ At a later age, perhaps investigate mentoring options in your area – even by someone who's neurodivergent too (and ideally, who shares some of your child's interests).

☐ If your child's attempts at social interaction are unusual, be accepting of them. Besides fostering your child's social confidence, this encourages others to do the same.

☐ Make sure you socialize in situations that can be got out of easily, without hassle or comments.

☐ Overall, follow your child's lead about how much socializing they can manage, taking it in small steps and observing how they're doing.

☐ Perhaps have a secret code your child can signal to you when they've had enough. This could be two taps on the shoulder or arm, or blinking at you three times (though it could be anything).

On 'de-sensitization'

When sensitive children are regularly exposed, against their wishes, to stressful social situations from which they have no means of escape, the effect isn't positive. Often, in our well-meaning attempts to 'toughen up' our shy, sensitive children, frustratingly they seem to get even more anxious, fearful, and negative.

Even if they seem to be 'coping' (perhaps after a bumpy, difficult beginning) we need to watch, a) if they seem regularly anxious, withdrawn, and/or overexcited, and b) whether they could be pretending/acting in order to manage in this social environment they have no choice about being in (i.e. are they 'masking'? – more on this in Chapter 11, 'Emotions').

☐ Be aware your child will need long periods of downtime from socializing. There is more on this in Chapter 3, 'Downtime'.

☐ Resist any urge to compare your child's social and communication styles unfavourably to others' for example, by admiring those who are smiley, chatty, responsive, and say 'please' and 'thank you' a lot. Instead, make it clear to your child that if they're introverted and/or their style is unusual, that's great – it's who they are, it's fabulous, and it doesn't need changing.[30]

☐ If your child is upset with someone, don't put pressure on them to have contact or make it up with that person. Your child should follow their *own* instincts about what contact they want, with whom, and when. You can, however, model not blaming people for things nor holding grudges against them – even if there are those you keep at a distance purely for safety purposes. It's great if your child sees that there can – and should – be such things as boundaries (and even anger or upset feelings) but without any blame involved.

Making friends

☐ One-on-one is usually easiest for neurodivergent children. It may be difficult, if not downright impossible, to make new friends in a group situation as they'll be too overwhelmed/overstimulated to interact constructively.
☐ Observe, when you get the chance, which other children your child seems to get along best with. And (at a time when you and your child feel strong and stable enough) see if you can arrange a play date with them or an informal meet-up.
☐ Many neurodivergent people like meeting new people in neutral spaces, as a) there's no sense of someone unfamiliar invading your private space, and b) you can leave easily when *you* want to. Perhaps therefore, if they prefer, choose another place they feel confident and at ease (for us, this was a local playpark).
☐ Provide some structured games and play. Games (if outside), like 'What's the time, Mr Wolf?', hide-and-seek, or similar – or if indoors, perhaps a board game. Participate (but using a gentle and light, 'non-obligatory' touch) in the games yourself if that helps break the ice.
☐ Lots of neurodivergent children enjoy working at things alongside one another, where you don't have to interact all the time.

Activities like handicrafts, artwork, modelling with clay, playing with bricks, or in the sandpit, can be great for this.

☐ Try nurturing selected friendships informally for example, by creating opportunities during the holidays to get to know another schoolfellow who they like, or spending time with the child of family friends, or a cousin – even if they're of different ages.

Socializing with same-aged children is actually not as important for a child's development as we tend to think.[31] Plus, if we try too hard to push friendship onto our children, they'll feel a failure if it doesn't work.

Considering all this, it's best to take things gently and slowly, without worrying too much, and with plenty of downtime in between social activities. Note: for a lot of autistic adults, one to two face-to-face interactions with other humans per week are perfectly sufficient to fulfil our needs in that regard!

☐ Don't discount family members and family friends from being your child's closest friends. This could include siblings, aunts/uncles, grandparents, or even an elderly neighbour and their cat.

☐ And finally, you are allowed to be your own child's closest friend. Yes, you! There is absolutely no law to say that parents and their children cannot be great friends – and this can grow as your child becomes older and more mature, allowing you to gradually ease off on your 'parental authority' role.

In school and other social situations (especially where you're not present), your neurodivergent child may tend to cling to one friend or 'bestie' as their point of reference. If you consider how overwhelmed and insecure they might be feeling, combined with the neurodivergent preference for one-on-one interacting, you can start to see why!

In this situation, nurturing an additional friendship/acquaintance for your child can be a good idea (if possible), just in case of mishaps. But again, don't forget the value of your child's friendship with you, their parent; as you're unlikely to be going anywhere anytime soon, this is one relationship they can pretty much rely on!

Group situations

☐ Children who find social situations daunting often find it easier, especially at first, to relate to others when there's some structure offered. It can be super helpful if the adult present coordinates some fun, optional, non-competitive activities, crafts, puzzles, or games.

☐ When your child is with other kids, and especially new acquaintances in a group situation, observe how things are going (try to do this in a hawk-like way, while appearing totally nonchalant and unconcerned).

☐ If all the kids are *not* playing happily, step in. Do this in as natural and friendly manner as you can, without placing focus on any one child or commenting on what's happening. Perhaps start with either a) introducing a more structured game, b) leading in an alternative activity, or c) simply hunkering down to play, or help play, alongside them (e.g. kids often love it if an adult opts in to quietly be the 'Lego piece finder'). More on what to do when kids aren't getting along can be found in Chapter 6, 'Communication'.

Directing dynamics during play

I see it as being like moving stones to assist a stream's flow. Soon (when the kids know each other and have settled into a natural positive dynamic) as the adult you'll need to do very little, and eventually nothing at all.

A little aside on how amazing it would be if we had other adults around, and teenagers, who'd be experienced in helping out in ways like this. But sadly, as things stand, I think most of us parents can only dream about such things.

In fact, society's strong predilection for seeing pronounced independence in people (however young), and the praise and admiration given to parents who don't need to assist their children, nor want or expect others to do so, works very actively against parents of children who need higher levels of input, protection, and support.

☐ In group situations, if anyone's having a hard time (perhaps feeling hurt or left out), step in and offer that person another activity. Maybe a game with you, a puzzle, or a story, or making some playdough (see Chapter 2 'At Home' for the recipe). Or else simply have them join in with something you're doing.

☐ Bear in mind group situations tend to be quite adrenaline-filled, and even quite stressful, for *all* children (not just neurodivergent ones!).

We currently operate within an inherently competitive system. Which means people (and especially children, who invariably spend a large portion of their waking hours in a smaller and more concentrated version of it) aren't going to naturally gravitate towards being kind, accepting, and cooperative with one another when alone. That they would/should do so is an extremely false assumption which leads to a lot of problems for a lot of children.

Organized, structured group activities or classes on their favourite subjects can be enjoyable for neurodivergent children (see 'Special interests' in Chapter 3, 'Downtime and Hobbies'). Only, don't actively expect them to make friends during these activities – they may, or they may not. Neurodivergent people are quite unlikely to see attending a preferred activity as a 'means to an end'. Generally, if we're dancing, we're dancing. If we're playing chess, we're playing chess. If we're making pom-poms, we're making pom-poms (i.e. it won't necessarily have occurred to us we're here to socialize as well!).

This isn't to say it won't ever happen – I have on occasion been astonished by someone nice talking to me or even, to my bemusement, wanting to spend break-time together! But it would definitely be better, for all concerned, if the parent doesn't actively expect it to happen.

☐ Note that autistic/neurodivergent people may find it easier to connect with *other* neurodivergent people. While this is especially true once we become adults (and have access to self-led social networks, etc.) this may be useful for parents to understand as well, as there may be options for nurturing such friendships and connections earlier than in adulthood.

'The Double Empathy Problem'[32]
This theory, elaborated by researcher Dr Damian Milton, examines how a mismatch in interaction styles can lead to a communication disconnect between autistics and non-autistics. Interestingly, this goes both ways! Research (the citations are given in Dr Milton's paper) has shown how non-autistic people struggle to read the emotions and intentions of autistic participants, very similarly to how autistics struggle to read those of non-autistics.

☐ It's best to assume (till proven otherwise) that your neurodivergent child won't want to talk with people (yes, not even you!) on the phone or by videochat. And if they're reluctant, don't try to persuade them. Other ways of staying in touch could be sending photos, postcards and letters, texting/messaging, emailing, and (for some) recording video or audio messages.

Parties and gatherings

☐ Arrive early at parties. This allows time to become familiar with the environment and means not being faced with an overwhelming crowd on arrival.

☐ Keep in mind that any difficult or antisocial behaviour is extremely likely to be an immediate response to stress and/or discomfort. More on what to do in these situations is given in Chapter 6, 'Communication' and Chapter 4, 'Out and About'.

☐ Have a secret signal your child can make to you when they've had enough. But don't rely on this – observe them as well.

☐ If you see your child become pale and withdrawn at social or family events, or start rocking/stimming, it's a good indicator they need to go somewhere there's less stimulation.

☐ Help your child find quiet space and time alone or just with a carer or friend during parties or gatherings whenever they need it. Note: autistic children may not be wild about being all alone in the midst of social gatherings. It's generally assumed autistic people are happy because we may opt to do it, but this does *not* mean we're always comfortable with the situation.

Misunderstandings, mishaps, and conflicts

Humans do have misunderstandings and conflicts – if we're close to one another, it's bound to happen. The important thing is, knowing what to do when it does.

In general

☐ Show your child your capacity and availability to talk openly and genuinely about relationships (tricky things, at the best of times), and to admit freely to your own vulnerabilities and mistakes. If your child feels understood by you in this way, it will come in very useful when they've been upset in a social situation or inter-action. More about this in Chapter 6, 'Communication'.

☐ Have some general, conceptual discussions in the family about overall kindness and empathy towards others – and possible al-ternatives to blame, revenge, aggression, and violence (more in Chapter 11, 'Emotions').

☐ Bear in mind that when children begin to go wild and start hurt-ing one another, they're invariably feeling overwhelmed, over-stimulated, and stressed – which usually includes feeling hurt and confused by the others and/or by the situation.

It's useful to have some strategies up your sleeve for dealing with situations of conflict with other children. The following points cover some of those situations and strategies.

If anyone's become upset and angry

☐ Start by making sure everyone's safe (bearing in mind that some-times it's easier to move others away from an upset/angry child than vice versa).

☐ As soon as practicable, get to the child and reassure them. You'll need to apply plenty of comfort, as they'll probably be feeling a lot of shame and distress. It's important to show you love them unconditionally, and don't judge them at all.

If you're seeing play that's getting a bit too wild

☐ You can state rules in a firm tone, for example, 'No hitting,' 'No kicking,' or 'No throwing stuff in the sandpit.'

☐ State to the children firmly what things are for, for instance, 'The sand in here isn't for throwing, it's for playing with and digging in.'

☐ It can be helpful to give information such as 'When it's thrown it can go in people's eyes.' And, if you're me, you may add a personal touch, 'Plus, it goes everywhere, and I *really* hate sweeping it up afterwards!'

The statements in the above three tips can be said firmly and even quite loudly (but *not* judgementally).

☐ If things get rough, and/or if there's a conflict, try some redirection. You could initiate an alternative collaborative activity – for example, 'Hey, we could dig a moat together and then fill it from the watering can.'

☐ Keep a very careful eye on any roughhousing. Be poised to intervene, and do so as soon as you are in any doubt.

Rowdy play

At any point when something looks painful or even just very unequal (e.g. more children jumping on just one child, or a bigger child wrestling a smaller one to the ground), even if they're all laughing, it's best to step in. You can say firmly and loudly, 'Wait a second!' And, once you've got their attention, '[Name], are you enjoying this game?'

If the answer from the crushed or chased child is 'No' (even just a tiny shake of the head), then the grown-up can say firmly,

'Games are only fun when everyone enjoys it. If there is any person not enjoying it, it's not a fun game any more.'

But if they *are* enjoying the game (this can just as easily happen), before letting them go on playing (especially if the game involves people shrieking, and/or saying, 'Stop, stop, no, NO!' between howls of laughter), perhaps get them to agree on a word or sign for when someone really means 'stop!'

☐ It's better not to comment on a child's behaviour or actions in front of others. Save it for a moment when, a) you're not stressed, b) there isn't an audience, and c) you've had a think about whether the thing needs to be said, or whether some positive redirection and leading-by-example may be enough.

☐ If your physical intervention becomes imperative, keep it neutral (taking no sides) and as peaceable and purely preventative as possible. (I've found myself standing between children who were trying to hit or kick one another, at which point it can get ridiculous, especially as I was cooking and had very sticky hands. It *is* good if everyone can end up laughing!)

☐ There's no need to make enquiries into 'what happened?' when a child's been hurt or upset during play with other children. Instead, focus on the injured party ('Are you okay? Where does it hurt?'), offering comfort and reassurance to them – and possibly (depending on the situation) suggesting a different activity, for example, 'Hey, shall we go inside instead? We could get the paints out!'

If focus *always* goes onto the injured party and how to make it better for them, instead of onto what happened and who's responsible, the kids (provided there aren't other negative factors playing in their lives) begin to a) resolve their conflicts

constructively without even calling an adult, and b) when someone is hurt, respond automatically, 'Are you okay?' (instead of,
'It wasn't me!').

I've been known to tell children (those with a marked tendency to gather around me chorusing their excuses when someone got hurt) that I'd only be interested in knowing 'what happened' if, for example, someone got bitten by a snake – in which
case I'd want to know what the snake looked like.

Stepping back from a situation and helping a child do so

☐ If at any point, despite your interventions, a child has clearly
just Had Enough, see if they want a story read to them, and/
or to have a drink or snack. Or suggest a quiet game or activity
together. Or they could help you in what you're doing, if they
feel like it (children may, for example, like being given simple
tasks to do as 'chef's assistant', helping you hang out laundry by
passing you the pegs, or similar).

☐ When there have been ruptures, make it clear by your demeanour
towards *all* the children that you don't think anyone's to blame
for mishaps or upsets. But *do* be aware you may need to navigate
carefully around any hurt feelings while doing this (more on this
in Chapter 6, 'Communication'.

☐ If you've separated children in the way I've described above and
brought one of them away to do some activities with you, don't
be surprised if the other child/children soon pop up, all eager
to join in as well. If this happens, be friendly and welcoming
to them, making it clear you don't blame anyone for what's
happened.

☐ But do, immediately after any rupture, keep a *very* careful eye on
how everyone's treating each other. The children need to feel
you'll keep them safe (even from each other!).

Lots more about disagreements and conflict resolution can be found in Chapter 6, 'Communication'.

TO SUM UP

To wrap up this chapter, the importance of our friendships to us, as human beings, is huge.[33] But our ideas about *what friendship looks like* may need to be adapted when it comes to our neurodivergent children, if we want to give them a chance of success at it.

CHAPTER 6
Communication

*Communication is the exchange of ideas, thoughts, informa-
tion, and messages – whether through talking, gesturing,
facial expressions, writing, or through our behaviour.*

Nurturing good communication within the family is vital, as it helps
to create harmony overall and makes for positive, strong relationships with our children.

In the previous chapter I talked about the 'Double Empathy
Problem', where Dr Milton, drawing from research studies on communication between autistics and non-autistics, illustrates how a
mismatch in styles can cause a disconnect in communication between the two groups – which, interestingly, works both ways! This
applies to *all* types of communication – whether verbal, spoken,
or behaviour and/or body language. He compares it to the way in
which two people with a cultural and/or language difference may,
through no fault of their own, simply not understand what the other
is trying to express. The result, all too often, is a breakdown in communication.

Some neurodivergent people may be unable to communicate through speech. This can happen either temporarily, in specific situations or for certain periods in our lives, or for some, permanently (note: this can be due to co-occurring conditions affecting the motor abilities).

Since human society has come to rely very heavily on the use of spoken language, this can be problematic – for those around us but, first and foremost, for the one who is non-speaking. The best approach is to a) look for shared ground, and b) find creative strategies for communication. This is far preferable to trying to make people speak, and/or leaving them isolated, unable to communicate with those around them.

In all our endeavours to communicate with, and understand, our neurodivergent children, it's essential we keep our focus on *differences* rather than on *deficits*.

In this chapter there are lots of tips on how communication within the family, and especially between its neurodivergent and neurotypical members, may be optimized. I'll try to explain how neurodivergent people may be receiving and experiencing things you're doing and saying, and how what they're saying and doing might be getting 'lost in translation' too. Bear in mind that kids also communicate with us through their behaviour[34] (which is *not* to say they're necessarily conscious of what they're communicating, how, and to whom).

I'll do my best to address a whole bunch of different situations families and children might find themselves in with regard to communication, and especially misunderstandings. It's going to vary enormously from family to family, so what I cover here is only ever going to be a tiny sample of all the 'possibles'. And finally, I'll look at some ways our learned communication styles may, at times, be actively working against us in our endeavours to understand one another, without us even being aware it's happening.

Communication styles

☐ Don't insist on eye contact. For autistic people this can be overwhelming, or even, on occasion, painful – especially if forced or we're reprimanded for the lack of it.[35] It can also take up all our focus, so if we're looking at you, we can't also listen to what you're saying. (I'm imagining my primary school teacher here: 'You need to listen! And *look* at me when I'm speaking.')

In exceptional circumstances, where a lack of eye contact may get unfavourably remarked upon, there are certain tricks one can use – for example, we may look at a person's hair, nose, or eyebrows. But your child should *not* have to use strategies like this too regularly. More on 'masking', and the dangers of using it habitually, in Chapter 11, 'Emotions'.

☐ Let your child communicate within the family in their own way. Don't insist on the use of words, and treat all modes of communication as equally valid and important. The more confident, understood, and listened to (regardless of what form that takes) our neurodivergent children feel when with their nearest and dearest, the more equipped they'll be to happily communicate also outside the family, and in different ways.

☐ Help your child out only on occasions when they *actively ask* your advice on how to interact with others and make themselves better understood. Give them information in bite-size chunks, observing their reactions and stopping when you see they're not absorbing any more.

☐ If your child is late to start speaking, and/or has trouble when trying to speak, check out resources on AAC (Augmentative and Alternative Communication) and Facilitated Communication. Try exploring different communication styles together (your child may be desperate to communicate, with you and/or their peers, and just be missing the means to do it!). More on this in the section below, 'AAC and Facilitated Communication'.

☐ Be aware that many neurodivergent people need a bit more time to absorb information. It's best to a) avoid giving long, fast explanations, b) allow your child plenty of time to react and respond, and c) not jump to assumptions about what they're trying to communicate or have understood.

Fun communication

☐ Try using some animal noises and non-verbal noises yourself (if you don't already). Examples? A 'meow' could mean, 'sure' – a 'frrrr' could mean, 'Aw, I really like that', and so on.

☐ Feel free to talk to animals. And to objects. Your neurodivergent child will most likely find this perfectly normal.[36]

☐ Communicate by text message with older kids. They may enjoy using images, memes, and GIFs (these can be great for expressing emotions and feelings, as well as for humour). Note: seeing pictures, for example, of cats, dogs or pandas cuddling or playing together sets off similar chemical reactions in our brains to real cuddles and play.[37]

☐ Lots of neurodivergent people express themselves through 'in fodumping' (talking to you at length about our special interests – and yes, it is a compliment!). It's great for us to find people who are quite happy to listen, and even ask questions with interest, as in these subject areas we truly feel confident – plus, it's just so *interesting* (who could *possibly* not be interested in four-wheel drive system mechanics?!). It's important to note, however, that a sudden spate of infodumping from your child may indicate they're nervous about something (i.e. it can be a form of stimming. More on this in Chapter 11, 'Emotions').

☐ Some neurodivergent people express themselves through creative means like music (perhaps rap or drums), art, and/or poetry and writing – as well as other creative outlets. This can, I feel, often be considered as means of communication, as well as an emotional outlet and source of joy.

☐ Ask your children about their dreams, and feel free to talk with them about your own. It can be a fun conversation, and it's great practice for constructing/communicating a narrative – as well as for memory recall. Plus, I find listening to my children's dreams can provide a lot of information about their state of mind, their worries, and their joys.

AAC and Facilitated Communication

The benefits of AAC absolutely need not be limited to children who are entirely non-speaking. Many children may find having other available means of communication useful.

☐ Try different approaches, seeing what works best for your child – bearing in mind it'll change as they get older and/or develop their skills. See below for more information.

☐ Alongside this, look for practical support and guidance in your area and/or online. You'll need to ensure your child gets the support they need, for example in a school setting (and the more you know about it yourself beforehand, the better).

☐ Avoid all forms of speech therapy or AAC that rely on rewarding or 'positive reinforcement' to motivate children, especially those that rely on withholding something the child clearly wants till they 'correctly' communicate their desire for it.

☐ Keep an eye on whether organizations, professionals, or schools are offering information on, and support in, a broad range of communication aids – up to and including methods where carers actively assist children to communicate.

Currently, many organizations and institutions have a policy in place excluding forms of 'Facilitated Communication' or 'Assisted Communication' (any form of communication requiring the active assistance of another person). However, many people have benefitted from these methods,[38] invariably using them as a pathway to more independent communication.[39]

For more information:

What is AAC?
https://www.communicationmatters.org.uk/what-is-aac/

What does a robust AAC system need?
https://www.assistiveware.com/learn-aac/select-a-balanced-aac-system. (This is a private company. I'm just pointing to their website as a useful source of information, rather than suggesting you should buy the products!)

Beyond the Basics: Core Consideration in AAC Intervention, Carole Zangari
https://www.youtube.com/watch?v=o8g5K_1LCks. Besides useful methodologies and approaches, Carole talks about the importance of authentic purposes, presuming competence, trust, and self-motivation in communication.

Where misunderstandings may occur

☐ Try to use direct communication – rather than inferences, hints, or 'sideways' communication.

> Neurodivergent children can get really confused, even distressed, at mixed messages and incongruencies (e.g. when there's a mismatch between a person's words and their behaviour). So, for example, if the person speaking to them is smiling and using endearments but telling them something they've done was wrong or bad, they may – okay, they may even have a meltdown.
>
> And it can push us right off balance – even to the point of panic – when others reassure us that everything's fine, when we can see/feel that it isn't!

☐ Be understanding about your child sometimes not paying attention, and about forgetfulness. (Just a note, though: if your child is zoning out a lot, and having trouble dedicating their full attention to anything, they could be dissociating due to general overwhelm. More on this in Chapter 11, 'Emotions')

☐ Using your child's name at the beginning of a sentence may be useful (or even essential) to get their attention. As a rule, though, make sure that at least 50 per cent of the time you're attracting their attention in a positive context: 'Hey Jamie, do you fancy a packet of smarties?' or, 'Lily, look, there's your favourite singer on the TV.' (We don't want, after all, our children to develop a dread of hearing their name called!)

☐ Don't make your child facetime with people, or talk on the phone, if they say they don't want to. They'd probably rather roll over porcupines than do this.

Limits and boundaries

Having habits and routines (and realistic, reasonable boundaries to support these), is both reassuring to children and extremely helpful to parents. The parameters of these will vary a lot between families, but it's important they a) serve a useful purpose, and b) work for everyone (if anyone in the family is miserable, it's *not* working!).

☐ State any rules aloud (without ever needing to get personal) in moments when it becomes necessary to do so. You can say, for example, 'No devices at the table,' or 'No jumping on the dog.'

☐ If your child is sometimes autocratic (dictating to you and other family members what to do and how to do it, without seeming very willing to try to see your/their side of it), try to ensure others' needs and wishes are respected too – and this becomes especially important when siblings are involved. More ways of implementing this are given in the following tips.

With great power comes great responsibility

It's important not to allow a situation to develop where a child is behaving in a bullying manner, and other family members are complying. It's not just a terrible experience for everyone else, but for the child themselves! This much responsibility is far too large a burden for a child.

☐ If there's resistance to seeing others' points of view, be firm but limit yourself to brief statements that say how you or someone else might feel in a given situation and observations/information about the situation. For example, 'When I get criticized, I feel deflated,' and 'It looks like your sister is trying to say something.'

☐ Make it clear it's fine to change your mind. Model this, when you do it yourself, by giving a proper explanation (and an apology if appropriate) to those who may be affected by your change of heart. This is an essential skill and will result in an adult who is strong and true, but also flexible about listening to others' points of view and responsive to changing circumstances.

Note: There's more information on the need to control and on inflexibility (and ways to manage/mitigate it) in Chapter 2, 'At Home', in the section 'Routines, predictability, and flexibility'.

Conflicts and disagreements

Healthy conflict management is both a skill and a process. Its length and complexity depend on the circumstances, the people involved, and the context. (Note: complex ruptures can take weeks, or even months, to work through.)

In equal relationships, both parties take their share of responsibility for the process and its outcomes. But in unequal ones, where one member is a child (so still learning and developing) and entirely dependent upon the parent, it's the adult who must take responsibility. You may be wondering, 'But if I do this, how will my child learn to take responsibility for their actions?' Predictably (you know me by now, I think), the answer is, 'Rest assured, they will! Because all the time, they're learning from *your* example.'

Here's what it looks like, in stages.[40]

Stage One: Rupture. A disagreement or misunderstanding, leaving a child hurt and angry (or indeed, both/all parties! But our role here is to put the child first – taking a minute to compose ourselves, if necessary).

Stage Two: Communication. Letting the child communicate as and when they need to, without putting pressure on them or making them feel at fault for anything. Listening to what's being communicated by the child (however it's being communicated), with compassion and without judgement. (More on how to encourage communication, for example when a child is angry or unhappy, can be found in Chapter 11, 'Emotions').

Stage Three: Understanding. Reaching a better understanding about the child's feelings and point of view.

Stage Four: Acknowledgement. This can be done out loud, as factually and briefly as possible, and in a way that validates your child's experience (leaving our own feelings and opinions out of the equation) – and observing the child's reaction to check we got it right. Examples could be, 'You felt annoyed because I let your brother speak but not you', or 'At dinner you were really hungry, but there was only stuff you didn't like.'

Stage Five: Repair. Putting together solutions and/or making amends.

And now for some tips. As usual, these are intended to be used only as and when they feel right.

☐ Let your kids know that their views and feelings *will* be taken seriously, and that you're amenable to whatever compromises and changes are going to be necessary for your family's wellbeing.

☐ Show them how important it is to you that everyone in the family is really, truly well (they don't have to just pretend to be!).

☐ Tell your child you actively want to know when they feel sad, angry, upset, or lonely. Even when they don't know why.

☐ Show your child it's safe to say what they think and how they feel, by, when they do so, not subjecting them to interrogation or offering any 'quick fixes'.

When we offer unasked-for fixes, our message to the person who's having a problem is, 'If you did this, or this, or this, you'd be fine.'

We may say, 'Why don't you just tell the teacher?' or similar. Only (since generally the whole point was that the child couldn't solve it on their own) they probably now feel quite let down by us – and hopeless into the bargain. Worst of all I think, they've begun to learn there's no point reaching out to us for help.

☐ If your impression is that your child might *want* your insights about a situation they're in, ask them, 'Would you like me to try giving you a couple of suggestions?' If (and only if) they give a definite 'yes', before starting you can add, 'And if you want me to be quiet at any point, or feel overwhelmed by what I'm saying, just make a sign and I'll stop talking.'

☐ If your child is upset about something someone did, don't ever say to them, 'Calm down', 'It's not that bad', or 'You have to see it from their point of view.'

While 'positive' messages sound great on the surface, their effect is to be infuriating and/or depressing to the recipient – as there's implied criticism and disapproval in there, plus an overall air of moral superiority.

If we're understanding instead, after a few minutes the ranting might conceivably become milder – possibly followed by a pause and then, 'Hmm, but I suppose from *their* point of view...'.

☐ While it can be great to brainstorm with our children to get their preferences and suggestions (see below), we have to remember they aren't *responsible* for finding the solutions to problems. We adults are the ones who have to gather information, evaluate how our child's doing (hence all the observation), and figure out what's the best course of action.

☐ If your child tends to see things as very black and white (and their own view as being the only correct one), point out to them gently, 'You and I are two different people – so it's inevitable that at times we're going to want different things, or see things differently'.

☐ When you have differing points of view about something that can't be easily reconciled, calling a family meeting can be a good strategy.

Meetings: brainstorm!

When we do this, we sit down with some paper, and everyone takes turns suggesting possible options and courses of action, and/or our preferences, and I write each point down without commenting on it – no matter how wild or unrealistic some of them may be!

Then, we go through the points one by one, discussing each option. Surprisingly, I've found it's the kids themselves who, when we get to their own slightly wilder suggestions, say, 'Well, that's obviously impossible because...' (giving whatever reason it is), at which point I gleefully cross it off the list.[41]

☐ Don't apply any hierarchy within the family to different people's wishes or feelings. Everyone's must be equally respected. If there's an occasion where you couldn't accommodate a person's wish or preference, openly say so. Often, surprisingly, a simple acknowledgement is sufficient ('you didn't get your preference here, I'm afraid'), and when it isn't, ways can be found to make up for them 'making do' this time around.

☐ It's better to simply state your feelings if they're obvious to everyone anyway, 'feelings' being things like joy, sadness, anger (but try not to be mad *at* anyone), upset, grief or fear. But try to avoid using words like 'disappointed'. Past participles such as 'disappointed' or 'concerned', even though they're technically adjectives, have this slippery tendency to put implicit focus (blame?)

onto another person and their actions, rather than keeping the focus firmly on our own feelings and experience.

☐ If your child asks if you're annoyed or upset with them, don't say 'no' if you actually were or are (even just a *little* bit, and even if you didn't realize but – now they ask – you suspect you may have been). Instead, be honest – maybe saying, 'Mm yes, I do lose my temper in the moment', or 'Yeah, I guess I was a bit!' But then make it clear you love them and don't blame them *at all* for whatever's happened. If it wasn't them you were annoyed at, but something else, state this too, for example, 'Aw no love, I was just really angry when that darned door wouldn't close' (or whatever).

I'm not angry! Sometimes we think we're not angry with someone – or indeed, angry at all – when actually we are (anger being, for some reason, such a taboo emotion that many of us plump straight into unconscious denial about it).

☐ When you've upset someone, don't go into explanations of how you didn't mean it that way. A simple acknowledgement of the hurt/wrong suffered by the other person (yes, *even* if it was inflicted unintentionally) is much, much better.

☐ Openly take responsibility for your side in arguments (and if your child takes responsibility at any point, follow their lead). A simple example is if your child says 'sorry' spontaneously, you can instantly say, 'Oh darling, I am sorry too' (or equivalent).

☐ And never follow up any 'sorry' with 'that you feel that way', or similar.[42]

Without being aware of it, a lot of us can be quite fiercely resistant to taking any responsibility in situations of disagreement or conflict. This, I think, is because of having thoroughly learnt (usually in childhood) that it can be a very, very bad idea to do so. Basically, we were usually *not* safe to do so – which makes it tricky trying to teach our children (and ourselves) that it's safe to do so now.

- ☐ Never use the opportunity, after a conflict, to explain anything further to your child, or indeed press your advantage in any way. If you feel tempted to do this (it *is* very tempting!), just be aware that it'll be extremely counterproductive.
- ☐ Never keep on talking about an issue or argument – or indeed, anything – if your child has indicated they don't want you to.
- ☐ And make it clear to your child through your demeanour that you aren't sitting there nursing a grievance. Note: if you do need to get some anger out, turn to the 'Anger' section in Chapter 11, 'Emotions'.
- ☐ Never tell a child that being hurt by a situation, or not, is 'within their power' or 'up to them'. Our message when we do this is a) they're responsible for the situation in which they find themselves (i.e. it's their fault, as they 'choose' whether or not to feel hurt), and b) (since it's presented as a solution in itself) that we won't help them – they're on their own.
- ☐ In a situation where one child's been hurt by another, place *all* your focus on making sure everyone's all right, applying your attention proportionately to whoever you can see is in the need of most comfort from moment to moment – and this absolutely includes the child who's squirming inside from having hurt someone else. Knowing you hurt someone can involve some really painful emotions.

When you focus your attention on who's hurt, you're modelling to your child a) how to genuinely make things better when people are hurt, and b) how to never resort to blame, reproach, shaming, or revenge. I'm a huge fan of finding solutions (I adore solutions!) and I'm afraid that inducing any shame or guilt in people is a serious impediment to finding any. More on this in Chapter 11, 'Emotions'.

☐ If treating others badly becomes a regular occurrence (in my experience, this happens when other areas of your children's lives are being really tough), rather than getting drawn into conflicts, you could try calling a 'Family Meeting' to take a collaborative look at some rules to put in place around how we treat each other as a base line.

In our case, when we were going through a difficult period (the children were around six and eight at the time) we sat down together as a family and made a big and beautiful poster called 'Family Rules'. The children wrote out all the rules we agreed on, and we illustrated it together.

The main themes were 'No name-calling' and 'No violence' (and definitely 'no kikking'). The children's final contribution at the time was 'Grown-ups: No yelling'. Hm.

We stuck it on the kitchen wall, and, for a time, it was quite frequently referred to.

If, despite your best efforts, you and your child are getting stuck in a conflict loop, bear in mind they may be anxious and frustrated overall or in other areas of their lives. Tips on how to figure out a) what's up, and b) how things may be resolved, can be found in Chapter 2, 'At Home', Chapter 11, 'Emotions', and Chapter 7, 'Learning and School'.

Enjoyable communication and word play

☐ Indulge in interesting conversations with your family members, for example, at the table or on walks. Make sure everyone gets a chance to pick the subject matter, and that you listen to all contributions, however they're delivered.

☐ Have inanimate friends. Go ahead and give some of your child's teddies, dolls, puppets, or toy animals characters and even voices (pretend, initiated by you) – perhaps they can tell stories about their adventures.

☐ Remember your autistic child might have difficulties with metaphors and figures of speech, and a tendency to take things literally – so try to explain any idioms or exaggerations you're using (and check for signs you lost them!).

☐ Perhaps have some fun using some very silly humour illustrating things like metaphors and exaggeration – to get across the idea that this is not actually true, but rather done to share a joke with people, or for super-special effect.

Silly metaphors

'Let's build this tower right up to the sky!' (Then jump up and down trying to 'touch' the sky, unsuccessfully.)

'That meeting made me feel like my head was being crushed by a heffalump.'

'Let's burn that bridge when we get to it.' (That happens to be my own favourite mixed metaphor. It took my kids a number of years to understand a) why I said it, and b) why I'd then hoot with laughter, every single time.)

More on fun play and interaction can be found in Chapter 5, 'Friendship'.

Cultural norms

And now we come to some things that may outwardly appear normal and unexceptional, perhaps because we're so familiar with them, but may hold more-or-less serious complications for neurodivergent people.

Facial expressions

We generally assume (strongly reinforced by advertising and media) that certain facial expressions mean certain things. Only, when it comes to neurodivergent people, these assumptions can be quite wildly wrong. For example:

- Neurodivergent people may do a blank face (the 'flat effect') when we're either terrified or excited – or when we care very much about something. Or when we're listening intently.
- We may laugh out loud when we're upset, disconcerted, or shocked (and this can include being told bad news, like that our cat has died. This may sound like a far-fetched example, but it happened – to me).
- We may stare straight at people when we're thinking about something entirely different.
- We may scowl or frown a bit (making us appear angry, grumpy, or sad) when we're just thinking deeply or focusing intently.
- We may need to look away from someone to fully focus on what they're saying. Or, in some cases, close our eyes.
- We may frown and/or squint habitually because of light sensitivity – making us look a bit cross or quizzical.
- We aren't (unless masking) very self-conscious about our appearance – *especially* when we're busy focusing on something. So, we may look earnest and serious during conversation, and not smile a lot (or indeed, at all).

- We may look sleepy, and our eyelids may droop when we're stressed or overwhelmed.
- And we may, at times, overwhelm you with our passion, excitement, and animation – especially around certain topics.

Pleases and thank yous

☐ There's no need to tell children to say 'please' or 'thank you' (this is especially important, in my view, in the presence of others). They're likely to feel a bit reprimanded or remiss, so the sentiment it's likely to produce (resentment, annoyance, shame, resignation – even if in small doses) doesn't really match the words.

☐ Trust your child *will* reproduce the words 'please', 'thank you' – and whatever other expressions your surrounding culture is accustomed to – when they've had it modelled with genuine sentiment. And (in my experience) when they do start doing it, they'll probably do it most beautifully and meaningfully (if only occasionally), quite melting everyone's hearts.

Greetings and goodbyes

It may seem odd to you (if you're not neurodivergent yourself) but your child might have trouble with greetings and goodbyes. When everyone else is hugging, waving, and wiping tears away, your child may be suddenly stimming, obsessing about a special interest, staring in the opposite direction, or have gone all blank-faced and dreamy.

To try to clarify: These moments can be hard for neurodivergent people because a) they involve a change (that person was here and now they're going, or vice versa), b) these moments are emotionally charged and intense (we might not register this consciously, but we can 'feel it in the air') so we may either dissociate or show signs of overstimulation, and c) there's often a sense of someone expecting something from us, which can be – well, paralysing!

So, what can be done?

☐ Remove any pressure to hug and kiss people on greeting or leaving. I'm a grown-up and I find hugging people when greeting very difficult and stressful. From my perspective, my body hasn't caught up with the situation, and now it's going to be squidged by another human as well! If you give me ten minutes to 'arrive', however, then I *might* be relaxed enough for a hug.

☐ Don't make any issue over whether your child says hello and goodbye or not (especially in the moment). Perhaps if the topic came up, in another relaxed and friendly moment together, you could say, 'It is customary...' and explain.

Gifts and ceremonies

☐ If your child doesn't want to take part in gift-opening ceremonies (such as at Christmas and on their birthdays), accept their preference without fuss.

☐ Don't make children write 'thank you notes' for gifts. Instead, you could – with your child's permission – take a picture of them playing with the gift or wearing it (or whatever) and send that to the auntie, granny, friend, or whoever gave it to them.

☐ You could (if you wish your child to start understanding about gifts) mildly say things like, 'Hey, shall we bring along the colouring book Auntie Holly gave you?' or 'I *love* this chess set. I'm really happy Granny got it for us.'

Neurodivergent children can get overwhelmed by being the centre of attention and the idea that people have gone out of their way for us (especially if that fact gets 'rubbed in'). Indeed, this can make us feel utterly crushed! I hope this goes some way to explaining why we can sometimes be so forgetful, and/or appear ungrateful, for things people do for us or give to us.

Jokes and pranks

☐ Neurodivergent children can be what others usually term as 'gullible'. Someone could say, 'There's a giraffe in the playground,' and we may answer, 'Oh, really?', or look out of the window with interest. So do make sure your child's on board with any jokes, and explain any pranks.

Note: this tendency is *not* due to weak intellect! We're aware of the unlikelihood of there being a giraffe (probably more so than our tormentor, actually, when it comes to statistical probability), but as we see no earthly reason why someone would lie about this, naturally we believe them.

Lying and deception

☐ Don't come down hard on a child for lying. Figuring out *why* a child might be lying is much more logical than punishing them for it.

We often set children up to lie without realizing it. The truth is we adults may only rarely, if ever, truly consider and respect a child's real feelings and reasons for things. So, most children learn to make up 'good reasons' for things. Ones that will satisfy the adults. Lies. (Note: neurodivergent children find this much harder than most. Indeed, this inability can get us into a lot of trouble. Rather ironically, now I think about it!)

One example is a child asking not to go to school. Child no.1: 'I don't feel like it!' (Parent says, that's not a good reason, you

> have to go.) Child no.2: 'I've got a terrible pain right here!' (Par-
> ent says, oh dear, you'd better stay in bed – I'll call the doctor.) I
> have a friend who lost their perfectly healthy appendix this way!

Self-deprecation

☐ When you drop, break, or misunderstand something, try not to say, 'How silly of me' or, 'Now *that* was stupid!' Instead, say something like 'Ah, now *that* didn't go quite as planned' (or similar). After all, we'd probably rather not have children learning about self-blame and self-deprecation.

And one final thing to mention in this section on cultural norms is that social customs (e.g. how people may respond to certain figures of speech, and how they may expect *you* to react in return – and what meaning that may hold) can hold an 'anthropological' sort of fascination for some neurodivergent people. It's a bit like learning a foreign language! If your child shows such an interest, you can impart knowledge in neutral moments and in an entirely impartial sort of a way.

Helping with problem solving and with your child's worries

☐ If you think your child is having problems in any areas of their lives, the best course of action is to spend a goodly amount of time with them. This will strengthen your bond and provide opportunities for them to tell you things. Ideas for nice times together are given in Chapter 2, 'At Home' and Chapter 4, 'Out and About'.

☐ If they begin to tell you things, listen. Just acting receptive is usually enough, though it can, at times, be useful to repeat tentatively back to your child what you think you've understood – asking them gently if you've got that right.

☐ Avoid asking (usually difficult!) questions based upon pre-suppositions or opinions, and/or ones that imply judgement. Examples could be, 'What did you hope to achieve through that?' or 'Why did you trash your room?'

☐ If your child appears to want to share information with you, but isn't managing, you can ask them, 'Do you want me to ask you questions about it?' If the answer is a 'yes', ask some tentative questions (perhaps starting with yes/no ones). Ask gently, interspersed with '*if* you feel like telling me this...', giving plenty of no-pressure time to react and stopping if they show signs of overwhelm or withdrawal.

☐ If your child reveals to you, or you suspect from what they're communicating, that their distress is due to specific situations or circumstances in their lives, be aware you need to be willing to start thinking about solutions. Perhaps even inconvenient ones.

More about what to do in situations where your child's having difficulties and challenges can be found in Chapter 11, 'Emotions' and Chapter 7, 'Learning and School'.

Extrinsic motivation

I've already mentioned punishment. But – to give you fair warning – I'm going to go further with this, and look at *rewarding* children, as well. I think most parents, instinctively, don't really like resorting to *any* forms of punishment (not even the withdrawal or withholding of a tempting reward). But the problem is, what are our alternatives?

Here's the thing – our instincts about it are 100 per cent correct, but there aren't currently many (any?) other options. And any alternatives are going to be a) far less straightforward and formulaic, b) scuppered at every turn by well-meaning relations, friends, teachers, and pretty much everyone else, and c) very hard to apply with any child who's become used to being routinely rewarded.

But what are we losing out on by functioning in this way? And is it worth struggling against the tide over (because believe me, it *is* a struggle)?

By now, research has shown that using any form of rewarding has the following effects:[43]

- It diminishes natural pleasure in a thing (like learning, or being kind, or playing a musical instrument).
- It significantly inhibits positive risk-taking behaviours, self-motivation, and creativity.
- It eats away at a person's trust in their own moral judgement.

Read on, brave parents, if you want to attempt this winding and sparsely populated route!

- ☐ Don't offer rewards (also known as 'positive reinforcements') to elicit certain actions or behaviours in your child. You're going to have to rely on your relationship instead, and to trust they'll learn by example. At the beginning it's going to be much more work and require a lot more compromise, flexibility, and creativity on the part of us parents. But long term, it will be worth it! I promise.
- ☐ When you want to give things to your child (presents, outings, ice creams, or whatever), feel free to *just give* them – entirely unconditionally. Besides being a huge 'feel-good' all round, this does wonders for your relationship.
- ☐ If your child gets pocket money, don't make it dependent upon anything at all. The money is simply theirs – they need be grateful to no one for it.

I feel it's the moment to make a confession. In moments of ex-tremis, I've tried to bribe – both my children, actually! Literally, as blunt as, 'Oh gosh, I'll give you £20 if you just try one drama class!' or other equally desperate ruses. And I have been met by both with the answer, 'Nuh, I'm alright thanks.'

On the dark side, I've never got anyone to have a haircut or attend drama class this way. But on the bright side, I thrive on imagining my kids as adults, in response to something like 'Hey, I'll give you a million dollars if you'll help frack this pristine indig-enous heartland', answering, 'Nuh, I'm alright thanks.'

- [ ] Try – just try – to hold off a bit on praising your child. Yes, I know, I can almost feel your astonishment (I feel/felt the same). I'm so sorry, but praise has some unexpected side-effects. Just like other forms of rewards (to any parent's horror on reading this!), it can have the effects of gradually undermining a child's ownership, self-confidence, self esteem, creativity, and positive risk-taking.[44] Before you despair, the next tips contain some ideas about what parents can do instead (okay, or 'as well', if you're anything like me and sometimes just *cannot* hold yourself back).

- [ ] When giving the sort of praise or reward that cries out, 'I love you' (e.g. 'How wonderful you are, how beautiful you are, how clever you are'), perhaps try instead, 'I love you so much', or 'I love hanging out together', or other similar ways of simply expressing how deeply you care for your child.

- [ ] When you're tempted to tell your child how utterly gorgeous/ beautiful they're looking, try to limit yourself to looking at them adoringly and perhaps blinking back a little tear.

- [ ] Don't give unsolicited feedback on any work or project they're doing. Wait to be asked for input.

- [ ] *If* you're asked for input, focus your attention entirely on the work (and not the child). Stop, look, and consider it. It's important to take some proper time over this. If you can't, say, 'I want to concentrate properly. Let me finish this and then I'll be with you.'

☐ When it comes to giving input on your child's work, sit down or get close to look at it better. Think a bit. Ask your child questions about their work, with true curiosity, and/or make neutral, observing comments, for instance 'This fabric is so soft', 'Those trees look a bit like the ones at the top of our road.'

☐ If your child has made or produced something, use/enjoy what they did without comment or fanfare. If it's for example, a bit of jewellery they made for you, wear it. If it's a painting, put it on the wall. If it's food, eat it with attention, tasting it properly. And so on.

TO SUM UP

We've come to the end of the chapter on 'Communication'. As usual, I hope one or two things may have been useful! I also hope that (for those of you who are not neurodivergent yourselves and are bravely trying to bridge the void and to truly understand your child) some of the information given here may help to shed light, even just a little bit, on our communication styles and how we may at times, from both sides, need a little 'translation'.

CHAPTER 7

Learning and School

If you know how to use your mind and imagination, you have a superpower.

A lot of our ideas about learning and teaching may come into question when it comes to our neurodivergent children. When we do things by standard methods, much of the time (truth be told) not a great deal of meaningful learning is happening. Besides which, anxiety levels may be rocketing – and often not only on the part of the child, but for the parent/s as well.

Many of us have tried and tried to persevere with our child's education and learning, only to find we just can't get it right – in fact, it may feel like what we're doing (so diligently) is all too often having the completely wrong effect. Panic may start to set in as the realization slowly dawns that if we don't manage to find a form of learning that works for our child, there's a very real danger they may just give up and withdraw. Indeed, many of us (to our horror, and feeling more and more impotent) see this phenomenon happening pretty much in front of our eyes.[45]

So, what are the alternatives to keeping on persevering when all our efforts don't seem to be working? Well (scary thought) we could use a different strategy. One that might allow our child to be themselves and to learn – and indeed, be *passionate* about learning.[46]

Learning – some general pointers

The following points apply to all learning situations, but note that later in this chapter I'll get to the often-tricky topic of school.

☐ Follow your child's lead, making sure they have what they need for their interests and hobbies (much more on this in Chapter 3, 'Downtime and Hobbies').

☐ Provide plenty of opportunities for your child's learning. Don't accompany those opportunities with any pressure or expectations – or even too much enthusiasm! – of your own, as the likelihood of it all going pear-shaped, if you do so, is high.

☐ Conducive environments are essential for learning at all stages of development. In each family and for each child this is going to look quite different – but lots of ideas are given in Chapter 2, 'At Home' and Chapter 4, 'Out and About'.

There's no need to force learning onto children – they're naturally super active, hyper-powered, self-drive learning machines! The question is, how do we help their enthusiasm and drive continue past toddlerhood?

☐ Assist your child in finding places and people where they feel relaxed and at home (more on this in Chapter 4, 'Out and About' and Chapter 5, 'Friendship').

- ☐ Facilitate contact with mentors, older children, and other role models. Especially important and precious are relationships with adults and older children who like and respect your child (and vice versa) and who connect with them.
- ☐ Avoid pushing your child into doing activities they don't like and aren't good at. This will damage their (probably already quite fragile) self-confidence. I know this can be tricky once your child starts school (more in the 'At school' section below).
- ☐ Don't talk about strengths and weaknesses (I know it's tempting to do so!). Instead, talk about your 'passions' and 'interests' and – on the other hand – things that 'aren't really your thing' or are 'not your favourite'.

When we talk about strengths and weaknesses, we're making an external valuation about which things are valuable and which aren't – and also about what constitutes being 'good' at a thing. My feeling is that society might be sometimes getting it a bit wrong when it comes to valuing things accurately – and, well, I don't want to risk unwittingly following its lead.

- ☐ When your child asks you for help, give it willingly. If you're too busy, and the thing can wait, give them a specific time you'll help them with it – and then make sure to stick to it.
- ☐ Don't be tempted into taking a 'didactic opportunity' when your child asks for help (for example by explaining things, or teaching/showing additional things the child didn't ask for). Keep it brief, simple, and relevant to what they asked.
- ☐ During conversations, listen closely to your child's interests and opinions (even if they seem weird to you). Respond in a curious, uncritical way, without bringing the topic around to what *you* think they should be interested in or learning about.
- ☐ Follow your *own* interests when you get the chance, showing your

child how much you enjoy them – that is, the process itself, not just attaining goals. And if it's a competitive hobby, show you love it in itself and not just for the sake of winning.

☐ When being asked questions, in particular repetitive ones, be patient. If your child asks the same question and seems fully satisfied with hearing the answer over and over, they may be checking in with their reality to feel secure. However, if they register frustration when you answer, you may be talking at cross purposes.

Talking at cross purposes

An example of this is my son asking about the treatment of animals. He asks, 'Why do they keep chickens in factories?' I answer, 'So they can sell them in supermarkets.'

Two minutes later: 'Yes but *why* do they keep them in factories?' We could continue going round in circles like this for a long time, and I could get exasperated, or assume he's not very bright.

Ah, or...am I not answering the question he is trying to ask me?

When I instead answer, 'It is awful, isn't it – but more and more people realize this and try not to support it by not buying the meat', he seems satisfied. Later, he asks me, 'Can we buy all the chicks from the factory, and set them free?'

☐ When your child's working on a project, don't say anything unless you're asked for input. Most neurodivergent people like to be able to focus their full attention upon a task and not be distracted from it.

☐ Don't think you have to stick to 'age-appropriate' material for your child's learning. They might be amazing at something unexpected or that they're not meant to know for another ten years

– and show zero interest or ability in something they 'should' have learned years ago.[47]

☐ Be aware and accepting around the fact that your child may need to be in unusual positions, move around, jump, throw and catch something, for example, a ball, or make sets of movements to cognitively learn things.[48]

A few ideas to try

In this section are some optional things you could try out, depending on your own child, family, and situation in general.

☐ Make a dedicated 'creative space' for your child (even just a table in a corner of the kitchen or living room) where there are pens, pencils, crayons, paper, and whatever other materials their current preferred activities involve.

☐ Drama/theatre games and activities can be fun. These can be fantastic for practising different roles, conversations, and situations. (And if your child is into trying a drama club, great!)

☐ Spend time outdoors, if possible, following your children's lead about what they like to spend time doing outside. More on this in Chapter 4, 'Out and About'.

☐ Have a 'dressing-up box' –containing capes, silly hats, animal masks, and so on.

☐ If your child likes acting, singing, and/or dancing but doesn't want to do a course, family activities of this kind can be fun. My kids went through a stage of making stage sets and puppets and 'acting' with those.

☐ Make up stories and songs about things. This is a great way of imparting knowledge, too, as for some reason, where a textbook might make us fall asleep after a few minutes, an adventuresome narrative has the power to keep us gripped for ages – and even to remember some of the details afterwards.

☐ Audiobooks are a great resource for learning – and indeed (though it may sound strange!) for literacy and learning to read too.[49]

☐ Your child may like watching movies with the subtitles on (I do this myself, as do many neurodivergent people – I find it helps me to follow the narrative), which can help in learning to read and/or improving reading and word recognition.

☐ Many kids these days learn to read predominantly through apps and games. Although I've let my kids take the lead on what apps they like using, I try to make sure they mostly have games that don't rely heavily on rewarding kids with prizes, or on in-app purchases or advertising (note: this often means paying a nominal fee up-front for a game).

☐ Making things visible with art, illustrations, graphs and so on, and even three-dimensional models, can be helpful. Science experiments can be fun too. Getting a visual and a '3D' on things can be really useful for learning and remembering information.

☐ If you've got space and the opportunity, you could try out some more structured games, like ping-pong, badminton, swing ball, and so on (in a fun and friendly style!). There's no need to be competitive – not in a serious way, anyway – especially when skill levels are very different.

About competition and pressure

☐ Try not to be too goal oriented, as rushing from goal to goal is unlikely to be the best learning style for your child (and plus, horizons have this annoying habit of receding!).

☐ Don't pressurize your child into taking a particular direction at any stage of their life. Let them meander and explore instead – and trust they'll find their way.

☐ Don't talk about your expectations of your child, nor your anxieties about their future or achievements. Instead, trust that things will happen as they're meant to, when they're meant to (I know this can be really hard!).

☐ Try not to correct your child a lot as it undermines their self-confidence and autonomy. Keep an eye on yourself if you think you might be inadvertently doing this (and especially if your parents did or do this a lot with you).

☐ Avoid asking your child questions you already know the answer to yourself (unless it's in a very specific situation such as testing them for an exam). Your child's sense of logic will rebel against this practice.

☐ Model failure. Don't be shy! Our children learn a lot from our ability to admit defeat sometimes, and especially when we find other ways to do things, or other things to do, instead.

☐ Don't put pressure on your child to compete against others. If they lose, they'll likely suffer because of how vulnerable and humiliated it can make them feel. And if they win, they may sense any hostility/resentment directed towards them and be sensitive to the pain of others – so they may not enjoy the experience of 'beating others' quite as much as expected.

What Is 'competition'?

Some things we often think of as synonymous with 'competition' (like motivation to achieve, pushing oneself to excel, feeling driven to do something very well or to reach or exceed certain standards within an activity) are actually not quite the same thing as competing. 'Competition' can be best explained as 'your loss is my gain, or vice versa' (i.e. another is required to lose for you to win).[50]

Even if your neurodivergent child is among those children who outwardly enjoy competing, perhaps observe how tense and vigilant, and at times obsessed, they may become over it.

Consider carefully:

- Have they observed how important competing is in our culture (and how you can get acceptance and respect for it – something they may have been yearning for)?
- Does it look like it's doing them good, physiologically and emotionally?
- How close friends are they with the people they are competing with and against?

If your child looks relaxed and happy, and seems to be great, loyal buddies with their team-mates and competitors, then I'd say whole-heartedly, 'Go for it!'

But if you feel ambiguous, maybe consider having some parallel, or alternative, outlets.

Fun collaborative activities and games

I remember when a friend first said the words 'non-competitive games' to me. It was after a birthday party I'd organized which had become a bit chaotic around the games – things like the egg-and-spoon race, three-legged race, musical chairs, and so on.

Everyone who cried (mostly the little ones) instantly got a prize, as I couldn't bear it – which of course had made some of the other children, especially the biggest and strongest, quite annoyed. Luckily, I'd wrapped *so* many prizes that those quickly became boring, and the children ran off down the field to climb trees instead.

A couple of days later, my friend gently asked me if I'd ever considered 'non-competitive games'. I just blinked at her (I was too polite to say, 'Oh, yaaaawwn!' – as I must admit, even the words sounded boring to me).

Not much later, I learned that there are indeed non-competitive (or 'collaborative' games) – lots of them. And astonishingly (to me at least) both my children preferred them! Not just a little bit, but they really, really preferred them. As did I. It was so much less stressful, as it was fun for everyone and not just for one or two people. And there was no need to spend anywhere near so much money on prizes.

Here are some ideas for non-competitive games and activities:

☐ 'Hide and seek' or 'sardines' – the latter being when one person hides, and those who find them must simply hide in the same spot as them until the end of the game when everyone's there together in the same hiding spot. It can get very silly and funny.

☐ Democratic treasure hunt – this is more work to set up than a classic treasure hunt, but it's worth it, since you'll end up with happy children who are still quite keen on each other. It works well for a small group and/or a mixed-ability or mixed-age group of children (note: ideally, you need to know who's coming beforehand, or at least the number of children). When preparing the hunt, write each child's name (or a number) on the outside of each clue. When each child's turn comes up, they open it, read it, and take the initiative for this part of the hunt. It's given me great joy to see the older children, all of whom can read and know exactly what a clue meant, race off happily in the wake of the smallest child – who's enthusiastically run off in completely the wrong direction.

☐ Building a hide-out, dam, or other construction – I've yet to meet a child who didn't enjoy making dens (also indoors) and hideouts and building dams in streams.

Lots more ideas for fun collaborative activities for kids, and for collaborative party games, can be found online.[51]

At school

Whether your child goes to a specialist school or a mainstream school, there are some things you'll want to look out for.

Things to look for in a school

☐ When they feel the need can children (even young ones) go to a quiet place such as a library or computer room?

☐ How much flexibility is there within the classroom environment? Can children doodle/sketch in class? Can they move around if they need to? Can they have their toys with them, and stim?

☐ Do children not appearing to 'pay attention' in the traditional sense (eye contact, sitting up, etc.) get accommodated and understood?

☐ Is the staff familiar with autism and neurodiversity? Note: it's important, if so, that they take a neuro-affirming perspective.

☐ Does the school have resources and support available for AAC, if your child is – either permanently or periodically – non-speaking? More on this in Chapter 6, 'Communication'.

☐ Would flexi-schooling (attending school for fewer hours/days per week) be an option if your child needed regular downtime from school, and/or tends to get sick often?

☐ Can your child go to the bathroom when they need to, without attracting attention or needing to ask? Is there a disabled loo and/or one that's equipped with what your child needs? More on this in Chapter 9, 'Health, Hygiene, and Fitness'.

☐ Is it obligatory to go outside with the other children at playtime, or can a child stay quietly indoors if they prefer to?

☐ Are there special interest groups or clubs available, for example, in the lunch break (or could such groups be set up)?

☐ Is there an adult in the playground? And if the school is larger, what's the ratio of adults to children in the playground?

☐ Do the adults actively intervene and participate, for example, by providing optional structured activities to include children who feel lost or left out?

☐ Is there a system in place where children help one another for instance by befriending them, helping them find their way around, spending time with them in the playground?

☐ Would a child who gets absorbed in a specific project be given enough time to dedicate to (and/or finish) it?

☐ Is there greenery and nature (e.g. grass, plants, trees – or even a garden) in the school outdoor environment? Is there a sandpit, climbing frame, slide?

☐ Are there any school animals? Is gardening or caring for animals in the curriculum? I know this is a long shot, but it's worth asking!

☐ Can the sky and/or greenery (i.e. any natural light and scenery) be seen through the classroom windows? This is especially important if the children spend the whole day in the same classroom.

☐ Are teachers approachable, supportive, and open to finding solutions to difficulties? If it's a larger school, are there designated support teachers and aides?

☐ Does the school emphasize competitive spirit and achievement and attaining 'goals', or does it focus more on collaboration and the wellbeing and friendships of the children and teachers?

Supporting children at school

We may wonder how we can best support our neurodivergent children through their school years, and what to do if there are problems.

☐ See if you can nurture one or two friendships for your child – more on ways to do this in Chapter 5, 'Friendship'.

☐ See if there is a teacher or aide with whom your child connects and feels at their ease – and ask to what extent they're able and willing to be there for your child, during school hours.

If things go wrong at school

☐ If there are problems at school, and/or your child is unhappy or anxious, approach the school staff to try to find solutions (some ideas are given in the section above, 'Things to look for in a school').

☐ Keep an eagle-eye out for whether your child's being exposed to cruelty or bullying. There is more about bullying, and warning signs to look out for, in the following section.

☐ If your child is actively refusing or just having a great deal of trouble going to school, you'll need to act, starting (even just as an interim) with *not* making your child go to school.

☐ If the school threatens fines or repercussions for non-attendance (I hope this doesn't happen, but I'm afraid in some cases it does) take your child to see a doctor (your GP, if they are sympathetic), occupational therapist,[52] or a counsellor/therapist who may be able to help you.

☐ Alongside this, explore your options. Go online to find relevant parenting forums (online or otherwise), and approach your school's parent council, if there is one – or any other local parents' groups you're aware of. Your local education authority (or equivalent) may be useful on the options available and your rights.[53]

School-induced anxiety or ABSA (Anxiety-Based School Avoidance) – otherwise known as EBSA (Emotionally Based School Avoidance)

Some children may show physical symptoms such as sore tummies and even vomiting or fainting. Others might just quietly ask if they can 'not go to school today' and become pale and withdrawn, and may develop tics such as nail-biting or lip-chewing.

> You know your child best and can keep an eye out, and make a
> judgement call when you feel it's about their wellbeing.
>
> A 'Guide for Parents' about school-induced anxiety is found
> on the Young Minds website: *https://www.youngminds.org.uk/
> parent/parents-a-z-mental-health-guide/school-anxiety-and-
> refusal/*

If your school isn't approachable, helpful, or flexible (note: it's very
important to know your rights here[54]), you may want to look for
different options for your child. In the next pages there are some
alternative schooling options.

Bullying, ostracism, and discrimination

Directly questioning children about whether they're being hurt by
a situation, or expecting them to spontaneously tell us about any
problems they're having, may be less than helpful.[55]

Instead, it's best to protect your child, as of immediately, from
any situations you suspect might be causing them harm (signs to
look out for are listed below), and then look around for solutions
that *work for them* and keep them safe longer-term.

The following are signs to watch out for in your child, that could
well indicate they're suffering bullying/abuse:

- aggressive and angry behaviours towards younger siblings, ani
  mals, or others
- outward character change (what's happened to my lovely, happy,
  kind son/daughter?)
- excessive controlling behaviours
- 'school refusal' (or ABSA/EBSA)
- persistent interest in death and/or suicide
- a new obsession with weapons, guns, fighting, and killing

- regressive behaviours (e.g. bed wetting, 'tantrums', panicking about being left alone)
- inability to trust others or make friends
- self-blame, self-hate, excessive shame – even self-harm
- extreme fear of being separated from parent/caregiver
- persistent anxiety, fear, and avoidance
- chronic sadness, depression, withdrawal and/or immobility (listlessness, aimlessness, and tendency to 'freeze' when afraid)
- persistent lack of self-confidence, feeling a failure and worthless
- persistent digestive problems, stomach aches, or headaches.

More about traumatic stress (and healing from it) can be found in Chapter 11, 'Emotions' and Chapter 9, 'Health, Healing, and Fitness'.

For further information
A lot more information about issues neurodivergent children may encounter at school, and ways to constructively navigate them, can be found in Luke Beardon's book *Avoiding Anxiety in Autistic Children* in the section on 'School'. Detailed information about the options available to families with slightly older neurodivergent children can be found in the book *Nurturing Your Autistic Young Person* by Cathy Wessall – 'Autism at School' is extensively covered, including provisions available for special educational needs.

Other schooling options

If your child is simply not thriving at school, you may want to look at alternative options.

Examples of non-mainstream school include *democratic or sociocratic schools*[56] and *forest or nature schools*. If it's just a question of needing a little more downtime, *flexi-schooling* can be an option (reducing the hours per week at school). And finally, if your child would benefit from it and your lives allow, you may want to consider *home education* (either for short periods or longer-term).

Much more information on alternative forms of education, including home education, can be found in Dr Naomi Fisher's wonderful book *Changing Our Minds: How Children Can Take Control of Their Own Learning.*[57]

TO SUM UP

Neurodivergent children can be amazing learners, full of curiosity, originality, and creativity (in their own ways) – *provided* the conditions are right. It might not be easy, but if we can create a truly conducive environment for our children, putting to one side our pre-conditioned ideas about what learning should look like, then great things can happen.

CHAPTER 8
Food and Eating

How can a thing so necessary to our existence, and potentially so pleasurable, sometimes become so complicated?

Lots of neurodivergent children have trouble around eating and diet. This can manifest itself in various ways:

- a need for control, order, repetition, and habit around eating and specific foodstuffs (especially autistic children and those with OCD)
- a lack of appetite, especially in certain situations (even prolonged ones), for example when nervous or in a state of hyperfocus
- limited foodstuffs that can be swallowed and/or digested (many neurodivergent children have trouble with digestion).

And more serious problems, should they develop, could be:

- digestive problems for example, bloating, abdominal pain, constipation, diarrhoea, vomiting, irritable bowel syndrome (IBS)

- eating disorders, such as binge eating, avoidant/restrictive food intake disorder (ARFID) (note: this can easily be mistaken for anorexia nervosa), and others.

Autistic children are more than three times more likely to experience gastrointestinal disturbance than their non-autistic counterparts.[58]

Stress and anxiety can affect people's eating and digestion patterns[59] (and indeed, this can go both ways, i.e. having chronic digestive problems can bring about higher levels of stress and anxiety). So, perhaps unsurprisingly, the autistic tendency toward gastrointestinal dysregulation has been – to some extent at least – linked to often having high levels of stress, anxiety, and sensory sensitivity.[60]

We may wonder how to practically mitigate these effects. Areas to consider here are:

- Anxiety levels overall: High anxiety levels can manifest in, for example, a need for excessive control around eating, lack of hunger or interest in food, overeating, and/or digestive complications.
- Physical and sensory comfort levels: Maximizing these will encourage a child to 'stay in their bodies' more. (Note: problems with interoception – perceiving what's happening in your body – can, for neurodivergent people, mean forgetting to eat until you're fainting! Or forgetting to drink until you have a blinding headache. And so on...)
- Agency/autonomy around eating: This will increase a child's sense of being in control and pave the way for a good relationship with food.

Some general pointers

So, how to implement this? (Note: if your child has already developed any of the more serious eating issues, such as ARFID, I'd advise seeking specialist and/or medical help.)

☐ Have relaxed, pleasant, regular mealtimes – but quite informal, without rigidity or fixed expectations.

☐ Give your child as much autonomy as you can, as early as possible. When they're still very little, let them hold the spoon or eat with their hands.

☐ Involve your child with the cooking, and even with growing food, if that's an option. Familiarity with ingredients and being involved in the processes (besides being educational and potentially a lot of fun, too!) give children some decision-making power and control in the process.

☐ Some kids love having a special plate, mug, or bowl to use at mealtimes.

☐ Have open, curious conversations together at the table – and even jokes, games, and stories.

☐ But while it's great to connect, don't feel conversation is needed at the table. Doing things together without speaking can be beautiful. I recall when eating with my mother, as a child, we'd often happily agree to read our books at lunch (we had special book stands for this purpose).

☐ Give a good few minutes' warning before meals, so everyone's prepared by the time you call them. For older kids, they could set a recurring alarm on their clock or phone, to go off five to ten minutes before dinnertime (if you're organized enough to prepare a meal at the same time each evening).

☐ Don't put any pressure (not even light persuasion) on your child to eat. Ownership for their eating should remain absolutely with the child. Pressure, expectation, and even feeling observed can very negatively affect a child's relationship with food.

☐ You can tell your children it's fine to leave what they don't feel like eating on their plate (I know, Great-Granny will be turning in her grave!).

Keeping an eye on whether you're full, and acting accordingly (by stopping eating), is an important part of developing a healthy interoception around food.

☐ Your child may have issues with textures, smell, and so on. If this happens (for example, when you are guests at someone else's house), simply say to your child quietly, 'No problem, just eat whatever you can and leave the rest.'

☐ If your kid looks like they're going to keel over from hunger when the meal's not ready yet, or they appear by magic in the kitchen whenever they detect cooking smells, put out some cut-up fruit or veg sticks for them to graze on (or anything that's not actively unhealthy and won't ruin people's appetites too much).

☐ If you have time, try arranging cut fruit and veg to form things on the plate for example, an animal, an emoji, or a house (or anything your talent and imagination extends to!). In my experience, this is a great strategy to get fruit and vegetables into children.

☐ Your child may eat things – for example, a whole packet of cheese crackers – absent-mindedly, without really noticing. You could help them with a curious, 'Are you enjoying that, love?' If they respond, 'not really', you could offer them an alternative – but if they're perfectly happy, leave them to it, perhaps adding a neutral reminder to 'just keep an eye on how you feel and stop when you don't want any more'.

☐ Some children may bite, lick, and even eat things that aren't foodstuffs. While this is fairly normal (especially in younger children, as they're exploring their sensory environment), if it becomes problematic consult your doctor (as it may be due to a deficiency in their body or diet and/or sensory/interoception issues). Alongside this, it may be helpful to keep an 'event and sensory' diary to try to understand what's going on for your child and what factors the habit might be linked to.

☐ Be aware about allergies, keeping an eye on your child's overall health and wellbeing. If they look pale and/or often have a runny nose, nosebleeds, tummy pains, skin rashes, or other symptoms, try experimentally removing things from their diet – perhaps starting with dairy and then gluten.

☐ If your child suffers regularly from tummy pains, and diarrhoea or constipation, try adding some 'probiotic' foods or supplements to their diet.[61]

☐ Sometimes, supplementing a healthy diet with certain minerals, vitamins or tonics can be beneficial – as deficiencies and imbalances can contribute to physical and psychological stress. You can observe if your child benefits from certain supplements by trying them. (However, if supplementing is done obsessively, and certainly if it's expected to be a panacea, I feel it could have a negative impact both on the emotional equilibrium of the parents, and on the family budget!)

☐ For younger kids, carry beaker-cups of fresh water (I noticed that in a lot of our photos, one or other – or both – the kids are clutching one of these). For older children, I've found a good way to ensure they drink enough water is to recycle and refill small glass bottles, and always keep a few of those in the fridge.

☐ Try to always have fresh fruit available, too, if your kids like it; make it accessible for them to grab.

☐ All this talk of healthy food is *not* to say you must always avoid unhealthy foods! I'd vouch for treats and nice outings which include things like ice creams, pancakes, yummy cakes, or a deluxe hot chocolate. Mm.

☐ Make your eating environment pleasurable – perhaps with low lighting, cushions on chairs, and a comfortable temperature (and maybe fluffy slippers or a rug if the floor's cold).

☐ If your child resists sitting up at meals, just sit yourself down and enjoy the meal anyway – not making an issue out of it and going for 'whatever works'. By enjoying mealtimes yourself, you're setting a great example to your child – besides getting some necessary sustenance!

☐ Some rules for mealtimes can work well. They're best kept basic and relevant to everyone. Every family will have their own things going on, so any rules just need to be a) realistic, and b) acceptable for all.

We currently have three rules at mealtimes:

No.1: Everyone has to stay at the table for at least ten minutes (to counter the inclination of the children to guzzle their food to get back to some gripping game or activity, refusing seconds – only to be hungry again an hour later).

No.2: If anyone's finding the noise level is too much, they can propose a 'three-minute silence' (using the egg timer). It's amazing how you can really taste and enjoy your food during that lovely silence!

No.3: And finally, my kids' favourite rule in our house is 'No one's allowed to eat anything they don't like' (and they love telling this to any of their friends who come over for the first time).

TO SUM UP

On the topic of food, it's important to get our heads around the *extremes* of the eating experience for neurodivergent people. It can be wonderful (so much so that our souls are soaring, and our hearts are singing). Or, due to the exact same sensitivity that causes so much joy, it can be an excruciating experience – if it's full of things that give us pain on a sensory and/or emotional level.

This intensity, I feel, could explain many of the problems we experience around food. And it explains why it's so important to ensure it's pleasurable for the senses, and a time for connection – with oneself, with one another, with our immediate surroundings, and (most importantly!) with our food.

CHAPTER 9

Health, Hygiene, and Fitness

It's important to have an affectionate and loving relationship with your body. After all, you have to live together!

In this chapter, I'll cover the topic of physical self-care – including things like hygiene, staying healthy, and being physically active.

I'll also cover some aspects of emotional wellbeing – which is, after all, very closely related to bodily wellbeing – and I'll also look at the potentially sticky topics of therapy/counselling and diagnosis.

Feeling good in your body

For physical health, we need interoception (being aware of what's happening in our bodies) and proprioception (being aware of our posture, balance, and position, through various internal stimuli). To develop these, we need to be comfortable and confident within our own body and in our environment.

☐ Give unlimited but optional access to physical affection and closeness (as much or as little as your child wants). More on this in Chapter 10, 'Physical Contact'.

☐ Set as good an example as you can of nutritious and enjoyable eating within your home. Lots more about this can be found in Chapter 8, 'Food and Eating'.

☐ Give and receive head, shoulder, and/or foot massages, if enjoyed (note: hand massages can also be amazing!).

☐ Get a metal spider head massager (if you have no idea what I mean by this, try looking up those words online). They're *amazingly* relaxing, ridiculously simple, and great for helping to relax someone who doesn't want to be directly touched.

☐ Try some yoga and/or dance, as this can be beneficial to both physical and emotional health. More on activities like this can be found in Chapter 7, 'Learning and School'.

☐ Having an animal, or having access to animals, can be a great source of feel-good energy, and can also aid in fitness (especially if that animal is a dog, or even a pony!). More on domestic animals in Chapter 2, 'At Home'.

☐ Provide information (e.g. with documentaries and fact books) about how the body works. Knowledge and information around this can really help people with interoception.

Hygiene and self-care routines

Washing and cleanliness

☐ Organize your child's bathing and showering around their own preferences. They may enjoy a deep, long bath with loads of toys and/or bubbles every few days (in preference to a shallow functional one every day), or they may prefer showering.

☐ There's usually no need to wash small children's hair with shampoo – not unless it's got honey and/or mud in it. But when you
do, it's important to find a way that works *for them*.

> In my experience, the phase of being terrified to get water on
> one's face is temporary but needs to be treated with sensitivity.
> Your small child may like to lie back in the bath while you rinse
> their hair with a beaker, holding their head up with the other
> hand. Have a dry towel at the ready in case of drips onto the
> face, and let the child hold a dry flannel tightly over their eyes if
> that helps them feel more secure.

☐ When your child/children are small, go ahead and take baths (or
showers, if preferred) together. Babies and toddlers don't know
about body shame yet and find it way much more fun with you
there as well! I got some very thorough hair-washes involving a
lot of bubbles when my children were that age.

☐ Try to make sure the room your child's taking a bath or shower
in is nice and warm. Put their towels and pyjamas on the radiator
(this makes such a difference!).

☐ Make the whole experience fun! Supply bath toys, a pile of
bath-beakers or just random plastic tubs (anything that can hold
water and be tipped). You can also get bath bombs, bubble bath,
or coloured tablets for the bath. Instead of, 'It's time for your
bath', it can be, 'What colour would you like your bath? Yellow,
blue, red – or hey, we could make purple!'

☐ It can be fun having goggles and/or a snorkel. Underwater worlds
are great! (At some point we had a whole Lego sunken treasure
ship in there.)

☐ To foster autonomy around washing with soap and shampoo in
the tub, it's best *not* to make it obligatory. You may find at the

beginning – when they first find out about shampoo, for example – that they're using interesting amounts of the stuff (either none or half a bottle), but this will settle down into a more regular usage, especially if they have opportunities to observe how you use it yourself.

☐ Use non-slip bathmats in the tub, and (if it feels necessary) a protector for the taps/faucets in case your child slips or could burn themselves.

☐ If your child doesn't want a bath or shower but needs their face and/or hands washed, use soft, warm, damp flannels (with a small blob of soap if necessary).

☐ When telling your child about hygiene and health, do it a) neutrally (you're just giving information), b) non-personally, and c) non-dramatically (any drama can create intense fear around things, especially for autistic children and children with OCD).

☐ A good way of imparting information can be doing it around your *own* routines. You can say, 'I'm doing this, for this reason' and so on (while doing it).

☐ Avoid using words that could be shame-inducing, such as 'dirty', 'nasty', or 'smelly' – and don't ever show disgust, distaste, or withdrawal away from your child around things like personal hygiene or cleanliness.

☐ Never talk about bodies in a negative, derisive, or critical way. Ever. About anyone's. Including your own. Body-shame is a thing children learn by example. Instead, feel free to do the opposite – say, 'Isn't human hair soft! It feels so nice when I brush it,' or 'Aren't toes *interesting*?' (wiggling them), and so on.

☐ Body parts have names (whether informal or medical), and I think we should use them, both for clarity and logic. I don't see any reason at all why, for example, boys' genitals should have a name at bath time, while girls' genitals might get called things like 'down there' or 'your privates'.

☐ Unobtrusively make sure there's access to any haircare, body lotions, or other products it might be nice for your children to have, especially as they get older.

Approaching puberty

☐ Start placing age-appropriate books on your children's shelves about what happens to your body – and to you as a whole person – during puberty, perhaps by around eight or nine years old.

☐ When your child is approaching puberty, there are some wonderful age-appropriate books for children on love and sexuality, as well.[62]

☐ At this age, a child's hair may start to need washing a bit more regularly. If they don't want to have a bath or shower every time, helping them do simple hair-washes can work. Use warm-to-hot water from the shower head over the sink or bathtub, with a stool for your child to sit on and a folded towel for them to lean on. In my experience, kids can quite enjoy this (use a firm-but-gentle pressure and unhurried movements). It's more work for the parent than them taking a shower on their own, but it's quite a bonding experience (besides serving a purpose!). And – in my experience, at least – it's just a phase.

☐ Be aware that, as an autistic girl, getting your period can be a sensory nightmare – as well as emotionally confusing and potentially shame-inducing, too. There is more on ways to support your child emotionally in Chapter 11, 'Emotions', and more on the practicalities in the following tips.

  – Have everything you need ready for when your daughter starts her period (earlier than you think necessary, just in case). Make sure it's easily accessible to her in the privacy of the bedroom or bathroom, and that she knows where it is. If she goes on holidays or sleepovers, for instance, discreetly put a couple of pads or period pants into an inner pocket of her bag, and show her they're there – just in case. Note: schools usually provide sanitary products in the bathrooms, but your child might prefer her own.

- Note that autistics may not get along well either with tampons (I literally shudder when I hear that word) or with those sanitary pads that have lots of plastic stuff all over them. Reusable cotton period pants are far more comfortable – and/or the most basic soft, simple cotton pads you can find.

Hair care and brushing, and nail-cutting

☐ Use a mild shampoo your child likes the feel and smell of, and conditioner if they have long hair.

☐ If they want to, let them collaborate in choosing the types of shampoo, conditioner, and hairbrush you buy (but if they're not the least bit interested, try different things and see what works best).

☐ Try different types of brush if hair brushing is difficult. A detangler or large paddle-brush can work well for long and/or curly hair.

☐ When brushing hair, use gentle, unhurried movements, taking care not to pull. Hold the brush at an angle with the bristles pointing diagonally *upwards* (so it easily releases if there's any resistance) rather than pointing *downwards* (digging into the hair). With long and/or curly hair, start with the bottom inch or two, working your way all round. Once all the tangles are gone from that bit, go up another inch or two and repeat. If the hair is thick, first separate it gently into sections (using your fingers) which you can pin out of the way, to take down and work on one by one. If you encounter serious tangles, hold firmly to that piece of hair near the top (being careful not to pull) and gently tease out the tangle – again working carefully from the bottom upwards.

☐ Try brushing hair in front of a movie or while listening to an audiobook, especially if it's going to take a long time.

☐ For long hair, plaiting it (both in the daytime and at night, if that's comfortable for your child) can help minimize tangles.

☐ Tell your child to let you know as soon as you're doing something that hurts them.

☐ Don't ever invalidate your child's feelings around hair-brushing, or indeed any part of a washing, hygiene, or personal care routine (it turns out, if you ask around, that this has happened to a *lot* of people when they were children).

Invalidation of a child's feelings, especially if it's a common oc-currence, can lead to serious problems with interoception later on. Not to mention they'll have absorbed the idea that if they're hating something, physically, then it's their feelings that are at fault and not anything the other person is doing to them (and they have to just bear it and stay quiet). This is not a safe mes-sage for a child to learn.

☐ Be careful when cutting nails, as negative experiences (such as pain or drawing blood) can impact how your child feels around this. I generally did it while my kids were occupied with watching TV (but first asking their permission to do it), spreading a towel out to catch the bits.

☐ Don't ever comment negatively or in a 'shocked' way about the state of your child's hair or nails. Limit comments to things like explaining briefly why you're doing things, for example, 'I find when my toenails get too long, they can hurt inside my shoes'.

☐ And if hair-brushing is getting tricky, you could have a chat with your child about the whole issue.

This is a re-creation of the conversation I had with my daughter when she was around eight years old:

Me: You hate having your hair brushed, right?

Her: Yeah (at the time I literally only had to hold up a hairbrush in her line of vision, for her to yell 'Ow!').

Me: But it does tend to get a bit itchy and uncomfy when we just leave it to tangle...?

Her: Mm.

Me: Hm...well you know, shorter hair *is* a lot easier to brush... Hey, would you like to look at some styles on the internet? Just to see if there are any nice styles out there? But of course, it's your choice. I'm happy to carry on helping you brush your hair, if you prefer to keep it long.

Looking a bit dubious about the thought of all that brushing, she agrees to 'just look'. Luckily, in this case, she found a shorter style she liked the look of (to my relief). We've had other similar conversations since then, where she decided to keep her hair long but then spent more time brushing it herself.

☐ Don't ever push your child into having a haircut. If they want to leave their hair longer, that's their choice. Their head. Their hair. Their choice.

☐ Before cutting hair, make sure you have your child's willing consent, and agree beforehand about the style and how much is coming off (making completely sure you have both fully understood one another, before you start!)

☐ If you're lucky enough to have a hairdresser (or a friend or family member who can cut hair, who your child's happy to have their hair cut by) then you're sorted. If the haircut isn't taking place at home, you may want to bring along a change of T-shirt and some antihistamine cream, in case they get itchy and/or a rash.

☐ If your child won't let anyone except you cut their hair (my case) or if you're good at cutting hair (definitely not my case), cover as much of them as possible in a large towel or sheet, tying it securely. In my experience, speed and distraction are of the essence – yes, the tablet (what else?). And be ready if your child has a sudden need to strip down in three seconds flat, to leap straight into a bath or shower.

Teeth-brushing

When things are tough, more expendable parts of the routine can be postponed (such as washing, hair-brushing, or nail-cutting) but this one – except very rarely and/or in periods of true extremis – ideally should remain.

☐ Gently and cheerfully help your child with their tooth-brushing. Do it for them when they're little, and then continue to do so even after they know how to for themselves, if they prefer that (e.g. when they're tired).

☐ As soon as they're old enough, give your child autonomy, while continuing to do your teeth-cleaning ritual together (remember, they will be learning from seeing how you do yours!)

☐ Try singing Mozart's 'The Magic Flute' while you're all brushing your teeth. It's fun.

☐ Let your child pick out a (right-age) toothbrush, bearing in mind there are some nice electric ones available for kids, too – and with an electric one, they may feel more autonomy. You can even get ones that speak or sing (your kids might enjoy that more than you do).

☐ Take your child seriously when they have problems with certain flavours, textures, or sensations, and try different toothpastes till you find one that works for them (this could even be a flavourless one).

☐ Give neutral information about dental hygiene, or the dentist can do so. One friend told me that knowing that her granny still had good, healthy teeth because she'd brushed and flossed them every day made her really take on board the importance of regularity in dental hygiene.

☐ Dental check-ups are a good habit to get into (both for you and your children). A once-a-year visit can pre-empt any more difficult or painful problems. Try to find a dentist known not just for their skill but for their gentleness as well (both with their hands and with their communication style). If needed, you can seek a referral to a specialist dentist.

Toileting

☐ Keep the toilet area as pleasant as possible in terms of cleanliness, lighting, airiness, and smells. Natural odours such as lavender or rose oil (used sparingly) can be lovely.

☐ There's usually no need to have a potty for your child, unless you're camping or the toilet is far away (i.e. for purely practical reasons); instead get a comfy reducer seat for your toilet and a footstool.

☐ When helping children (whether with nappies or the toilet) there's no need to comment on what you're seeing or talk about their bowel movements or their toilet habits. Either a friendly silence, or a chat about something interesting to you both, I think makes for a nicer experience all round.

☐ Having said this, of course you can ask about whether something is comfortable or working for them (e.g. if the nappy is too tight, if it's comfortable, etc.).

Transitioning from nappies

☐ Don't put any pressure on your child when introducing them to the toilet.

☐ Note that children appear to never, ever want to learn to go to the toilet – showing literally no interest – and then suddenly, to their parents' astonishment, they do so out of nowhere (this could even happen when spending time on holiday in a different environment, or when/after interacting or spending time with some older children, for example).

☐ Let your child see you using the toilet. And feel free to say things like, 'Oh, I need a poo!', and then they'll (perhaps slightly bemused) see you heading quickly in that direction.

☐ Feel free to have characters going to the toilet for example, in stories, games, and drawings, or perhaps the dolls if you have a dolls house, maybe with a mini-stool next to their mini-toilet and a couple of mini-*National Geographics*.

☐ Take every opportunity to have your child not wear a nappy (does your kitchen have tiles, not a carpet?). They'll quickly become aware of when they go, and then – gradually – also of *when* they need to go (but if you do this, just make sure you're close by, to observe and clean up – in a friendly and relaxed manner and without any fussing).

☐ Be aware that children, especially neurodivergent ones, may have a lot of trouble coming to terms with this strange, wet, growling beast that we call a toilet. Just because as adults we're used to it doesn't mean we can't try to imagine it through the eyes of a child!

Here are some of the toilet fears and worries I, and others, have experienced.

- Might a snake or beasties come out of there? (In which case no wonder I don't want to sit on it!)
- Will it overflow when I flush? And if not, why not?
- It just feels so weird to sit on a hole. And it's cold!
- Might it swallow me up? Or might I fall in?

☐ In a neutral time and place (i.e. when no one's feeling any pressure or anxiety), find a short video on how a toilet works. Or, if you're able, you could even draw your child a diagram.

Once out of nappies

☐ Help your child by watching them for any signs they need to go, and then gently prompting them (they may shift to and fro in their chair or from foot to foot, and/or have a tensed-up, worried look). Neurodivergent people can have particular trouble with interoception, and especially when occupied in another activity – so we may be entirely unaware of needing the toilet until it's very, very urgent!

☐ Never, ever become angry and/or disapproving at mistakes or accidents, especially when in strange places. This can hurt and shame a child more than we can possibly imagine.

☐ Be aware that (for example when on outings and there's only one place and time to go to the toilet) an observed child may find it very hard to eliminate. The fact they're being observed, and there's pressure, means their body simply won't cooperate. So, a) try to not put pressure on them, and b) carry a nappy in your bag, just in case – and some tissues. Even children who don't wear nappies any more can, if necessary, go in one if there's no other option available.

☐ Make sure to never show disgust, disapproval, or impatience over anything toilet related. It's vital not to evoke shame around toilet use and eliminating, as this has the potential to create problems, including quite serious medical ones, later on.

☐ Keep cleaning your child after poos for just as long as they want you to do so.

☐ Be aware some children don't like the feel of toilet roll, as it can feel scratchy and might feel icky to 'smear stuff around'. If you have a bidet, this can be an option if your child prefers it, or you could try using a shower head and warm water.

☐ Fold the toilet paper rather than scrunching it up in a ball (which uses a lot of paper and can be scratchy).

☐ Try using a little warm water on a wad of paper for any stubborn soiling.

☐ When your child indicates they want to try cleaning themselves, let them, while refraining from making observations and suggestions (unless asked).

☐ If your child actively asks you about cleaning themselves, explain it to them – as briefly and neutrally as possible.

☐ I'd advise not commenting on the amount of toilet roll they're using. Just wide-eye it, and then (sigh) deal with it, perhaps with the aid of two or more flushes and a rubber glove. I genuinely think that's better than risking invoking shame in your sensitive child. And again, don't worry, as they will eventually get the quantities right!

☐ Finally, if your child shows a bit too much interest in their faecal matter, don't panic! This can happen for various reasons – such as sensory issues, need for control, or even simple exploring. (However, it can also happen for medical reasons, especially if the child is showing signs of any pain or discomfort around their digestion and/or eliminating – and if you suspect this, see a doctor.) Helpful information on why faecal smearing may happen, and what to do if it does, can be found on the 'Bladder and Bowel UK' website.[63]

Going to the toilet alone

☐ Let your child go to the toilet alone just as soon as they wish to do so. If they ask for the door closed and you to stay outside, leave it closed (i.e. do not walk in on them, however much you're itching to do so, as you wait expectantly outside).

> In public places, your child's new toilet independence may leave you quite anxious. Perhaps tell them you'll hold the door closed in preference to them locking it (but don't look in on them unless they call for you to come in). Check the toilet before your child goes in, if you get the chance – cleaning the seat with wipes/tissues and making sure there's toilet paper. If you're in the UK, you can get a set of RADAR keys[64] to have greater access to disabled loos when you're out and about. And if there aren't disabled toilets, people are *usually* pretty tolerant about parents and children taking priority and going into other-sex bathrooms.

☐ When your child's going off to the toilet, having proudly learned to go by themselves, and if you're on good, friendly terms with them (and – important – only if you're alone together) you could say a brief, 'Hey, remember to flush afterwards!'

☐ However, I'd advise not telling your child to go back and flush the toilet if they haven't remembered to do so. There's absolutely no need to make an issue out of it (and anyway, at this point you're standing there, and they've gone off). They will eventually learn to do it by themselves.

☐ Be aware neurodivergent children may have a strong aversion to going to the toilet in places other than home (including school). If the school has options for using a private bathroom (i.e. *not* cubicles), and/or has a separate disabled toilet, this could improve the situation. You can also try to get your child up and breakfasted early enough for them to have a bowel movement *before* going off to school. If they don't (and you know this is a problem for your child) maybe put some indigestion relief tablets in their schoolbag and ask teachers to be on the alert for signs of discomfort. If you'd like the school to call you when they see your child suffering like this, make sure you let them know (perhaps repeatedly) you actively want them to.

Hurts, pain, and minor illnesses

☐ When your child is hurt, focus *only* on making things better for them (i.e. it's not about stopping them crying, avoiding inconvenience, or not attracting attention). More about things that might work are given in the following tips.

☐ Believe your child about their experience – and validate it. We should never, ever say things like, 'But it can't hurt *that* much.'

☐ Kiss children's hurts better, if they like that. It's astonishing, but it can really work (indeed, it's known scientifically that the placebo effect works – so why not kisses?).

☐ There are various ritual gestures can make little hurts better. Some ice, or a plaster (perhaps with some pain-free antiseptic cream).

☐ Offer hugs if wanted, or (for smaller children) being picked up and carried for a bit, if they've been shaken by a fall or a cut.

☐ But don't make a big/loud fuss, especially in front of other people. Note that neurodivergent children are often averse to having people's attention directly on them – and this applies especially when we're feeling hurt and vulnerable.

☐ Due to difficulties with interoception, some children may not notice when they've hurt themselves. Adults present need to be aware of this, and vigilant around it. Every child is different, but signs (if the hurt is not immediately obvious) could include hyperactivity, nervous laughter, stimming – or else, for some, withdrawal and listlessness, paleness and/or wide/sunken eyes.

☐ When a child is ill, offer lots of comfort and nurture. This should consist both of *physical* care and comfort (covered, to some extent, in the following tips), and *emotional* support. More tips about effectively communicating your compassion to your child can be found in Chapter 6, 'Communication'.

☐ Don't insist on things like a temperature as 'proof of illness'. My take is, if a child feels awful enough to feign illness, then they *are* unwell (perhaps just in a slightly different way). For me, whether a feeling of malaise is in the mind, body, or emotions, is of secondary importance. I want my children to never feel they need to lie to me, prevaricate, or exaggerate to be believed about not feeling well and/or to get some downtime or a bit of nurturing.

☐ When something hurts, try offering a shoulder, head, or foot massage (or brushing the child's hair or scratching their back, if that's usually enjoyed). Sometimes this can bring awareness to a place in the body where something more pleasurable and less painful is happening. (But note: the child may not want to be touched.)

☐ Hot water bottles or heat pads can help a lot with things like sore muscles, a sore back, or a sore tummy.

☐ I've found my sick children usually prefer to be in the room where I am, rather than being alone in their bedroom. We have a sofa in our kitchen, and when they're not well both my children like to lie on that while I potter about for example, cooking or working on my laptop at the counter.

☐ I think it's usually fine to use painkillers at the recommended dosages (whether children's paracetamol or ibuprofen). When painkillers are available, I figure, why suffer if you don't have to? But I feel it's important not to use them to carry on with 'life as usual'. Instead, it's best to lie down, let the body and mind rest, and generally take it easy. (Note: aspirin should not be used for children under 16, and ibuprofen shouldn't be used for ailments which include skin lesions, such as chickenpox, as it increases the risk of bacterial infection).

☐ Hot baths are great for sore muscles, for example, the day after doing sports or other forms of exercise.

☐ If you are ever in doubt about anything to do with pain and physical problems, take your child to see a doctor. It's best to err on the side of caution, even if it's just to set your mind at rest.

Physical health, fitness, and sports

☐ Try to spend some time outside every day. Indeed, on nice days when you (or another willing family member) are free, little outings are a great way to keep fit.

☐ If you're lucky enough to have any woods, parks, or beaches accessible, see if you can make trips there a part of your weekly routine. More about this in Chapter 4, 'Out and About'.

☐ Having a dog (only if your life permits), can be great for getting everyone out of doors at regular intervals. More about having animals in Chapter 2, 'At Home'.

☐ If your child isn't keen on the outdoors, experiment with things like 'a piggy-back to the playpark' or, 'going on an adventure together' (maybe packing a picnic box). Often, it's the way we frame things that makes all the difference!

☐ There is no need to make your neurodivergent child do any competitive and/or structured sports unless they actively want to.

☐ As an alternative to sport or a structured course (if your child isn't keen on the idea) see if there are other ways you could encourage your child's interests. If, for example, they love swimming, find a pool that has recreational swimming hours, and go along together (preferably, if possible, at times when the pool isn't too busy). And if they have swim props and toys, so much the better.

☐ If your child does, on the other hand, love structure (and some adore sports, including team ones) try to find local clubs or sports centres where the emphasis isn't only on performance and competing, but on collaboration and camaraderie too.

Medication

At times, medication can be useful to help reduce a child's stress, overwhelm, and anxiety or overstimulation, to a level where recovery and healing (in a safe environment) can start to happen.

There are negatives, however:

- risk of dependency
- risk of undesired side-effects
- reduced connection with one's own feelings, emotions, instincts, and natural rhythms (though, on the other side, this also means they can reduce anxiety and hypervigilance)
- reduced effectiveness over time.

Any medication, therefore, ideally should be assisting the transition to a better place – as opposed to becoming a more permanent feature of a child's life.

☐ Before medicating a child, try to examine carefully (and as objectively as possible) the environment they're functioning within – and specifically, whether you think their problems may potentially be alleviated in other ways.

☐ First, if it's feasible in your situation, try other routes such as therapy, lifestyle changes, and/or putting in place a healing time and process for your child. There is more on therapy in the next section, and more about the healing process can be found in Chapter 11, 'Emotions'.

☐ If you opt for medication, see what you can find out about the medication/s your child is going to be taking – perhaps researching online, reading case studies, and asking those with experience (and/or a therapist or doctor).

☐ Talk to your child about the medication – what it is, what it does, and why (and for how long) the doctor is recommending its use.

☐ Alongside any medication, try to think of changes that could be made, in a near-as-possible future, to make things easier for your child in terms of their environment and lifestyle. Talk with your child about this, too – keeping them informed about your thoughts around it.

☐ Keep your child on as low a dosage as you can and, if possible, only medicate when you feel it's necessary.

☐ Unless medications are specifically designed to work together, have your child only take one type at a time.

☐ Carefully document usage and dosage, and how your child is responding.

☐ Avoid both long-term use of medications, and increasing the dosage if the effects seem to lessen.

Therapy

When finding a therapist

☐ Make sure any therapist you're considering is registered with the regulatory body in your country and look at their website for information about their approach.

☐ Avoid therapists who use behaviourist approaches. These may have been proven to 'work' in autism and ADHD, but (though many in the mainstream, and indeed many professionals too, are unaware of this) often enormously to the detriment of the individuals receiving the treatment. Many adult autistic people will testify to this based on their first-hand experiences. The children's behaviour may outwardly improve, but their internal struggles and longer-term problems do quite the opposite.[65] Terms to look out for include 'ABA' (applied behaviour analysis) and 'PBS' (positive behaviour support), but the main features to look for are a) whether they use rewards to 'motivate' children, and b) if the main focus is changing a child's behaviour.

☐ Therapists who may be of the greatest help are those who a) don't adhere to any one technique or ideology, b) recognize that many of our, and our children's, difficulties stem from our personal experiences, and c) are familiar with trauma-informed approaches.[66]

☐ See if you can find a therapist who uses 'play therapy' rather than just talk therapy (the latter is likely to have very limited effectiveness, especially for younger children).

☐ If you're interested in taking the route of finding a neurodivergent therapist (which can, in some cases, work well for neurodivergent people – see 'the double empathy problem'[67]), there are sources available for this (see below).

UK: The Association of Neurodivergent Therapists *https://neurodivergenttherapists.com/*

USA and International (including Canada, Ireland, and Australia): Neurodivergent Therapists *https://ndtherapists.com/*

General information about therapeutic and education practices for neurodivergent people can be found at the 'Therapist Neurodiversity Collective, Inc.™' website, *https://therapistndc.org/*

When starting with a therapist

☐ Start with an informal chat, perhaps just you and the therapist. Pay attention to the impression you're getting overall and how you come away feeling.

☐ Ask yourself if the therapist a) seems interested in your child as a whole person, and b) takes the child's needs and feelings seriously (i.e. it's important they don't think your child needs to be 'fixed').

☐ If you've come away with a positive impression, make an appointment for the therapist and your child to meet. This should be done with your child's knowledge and, ideally, their consent as well.

☐ Be open with your child about if you or people you know have received therapy – as the more we treat counseling and therapy as perfectly fine and normal, and something that many people may do for different reasons and at different points in their lives, the more natural it will feel to our child to be doing it too.

Very great care must be taken not to give your child the impression *they* are the problem. Unfortunately, even the act of taking a child to a 'doctor' implies there's something wrong with them, which can lower their self-esteem and potentially increase distrust and withdrawal. This is no one's fault; it is rather a cultural bias (anyone with 'problems' tends to be stigmatized). But this sad reality means any therapy or proposals about therapy must be very delicately, carefully, and sensitively done.

☐ Once your child has been to the therapist, observe them closely but unobtrusively. Note any changes. Are they pale, edgy, anxious, tense? (Note: angry and sad feelings coming up once therapy begins can, rather confusingly, indicate that some difficult or 'stuck' things/feelings are starting to shift. But do trust your instinct if you think anything's amiss.)

☐ After sessions, or in the next day or so, try to arrange spending a little time with your child, doing things you both like together. Perhaps even an outing if it's hard to find privacy at home.

☐ Don't directly ask your child about the session/s, but do make sure they know you'd listen if they wanted to talk about it.

☐ If your child doesn't want to continue with the therapist after trying a session or two, let them stop.

Note: If your child has a negative reaction to a certain therapist or therapy style, the chances of them being converted by 'more exposure' aren't very high. It's probably better to stop, give it a break for a while, and then (if it feels right and they accept it) try a different therapist.

Hospital

☐ For hospital visits, especially overnight ones, make sure you let the staff know that your child is autistic/neurodivergent or has ADHD, and give them any important information about your child (for example, doctors may ask children 'how painful' things are – and they may need to know this can be far from indicative, for autistic people). Ask doctors and nurses to write down important things such as this in your child's notes, but do also keep speaking up about any important points.

☐ If there's anything you foresee is going to be a problem for your child, but the doctors and nurses may be unaware of it, say something (e.g. if you've seen the nurse on the ward is a man, but you know your daughter would prefer any physical examination to be done by a woman).

☐ Emphasize the importance of you, or another close family

member, staying with your child during medical procedures and examinations.

☐ Ask to be informed beforehand about what's happening and what's going to happen. You can then give information in an understandable and palatable way to your child, if you sense they haven't fully understood.

☐ If there's a general anaesthetic involved (and you're not allowed into the surgery room) make certain you're present when your child 'goes under' *and* when they wake up.

☐ If there's any visit to a hospital, if there's the chance I put my child's blanket, favourite pillow, teddy bear and toothbrush in an overnight bag – just in case! If you've time include some sandwiches and a flask of something to drink, as you probably won't want to leave your child to go and find a cafeteria. Having a tablet or laptop with some movies on it can also be handy (and a long HDMI cable in case there's a TV screen in the room).

Things that are going to be painful

☐ When your child needs an injection, or a drip putting in, or a plaster taken off (basically, anything painful), first, with the doctor or nurse's help, make sure they know exactly what's about to happen.

☐ If your child has expressed they aren't ready, give them a few moments to prepare themselves mentally – perhaps encouraging them to focus on their breathing, and/or giving a hand massage to relax them.

☐ If your child is okay with holding still, simply be present and reassuring.

☐ Hold your child's free hand gently but firmly (the doctor will let you do this, but you may need to ask them as they'll be quite busy doing their job).

☐ It can help to suggest looking out of the window or at the TV, or a picture book – whatever's available. And then, in a calm and gentle tone, describe things you see there – a bird flying past, or people eating sandwiches. Or (if your child is okay with eye contact), you can just gaze into each other's eyes. While doing this, focus on breathing calmly, relaxing, and imagining a strong love and reassurance flowing from you into your child.

☐ But if your child needs to be held still at any point (this may especially be the case for smaller children), it may be better if you can do it, rather than a doctor or nurse – but only provided you can stay present, calm, and compassionate. If you feel you cannot, let the staff do this while you hold your child's hand and try to reassure them in the ways I've described above.

☐ While holding your distressed child, or holding their hand, reassure them and recognize their pain, keeping your voice low and compassionate (you could say things like, 'I know – it hurts – but you're doing amazing,' and so on – and then at the end, 'You did it! It's finished!' and give them a hug, if they want that).

☐ After any procedure your child has clearly found difficult, don't ever say, 'You see, it wasn't that bad!' And if a doctor or nurse does it, roll your eyes at your kid to let them know what you think of the comment (and/or say afterwards to them, 'I wonder how they know it "wasn't that bad"? Maybe they're telepathic?').

☐ If your child has had to be held still by force, note this will have had an impact on their trust in you, and in human connection in general, so some repair work will be needed. There's more on repair and emotional healing in Chapter 11, 'Emotions'.

☐ Finally, if your child needs to spend time in hospital, remember that it's not just draining for them, but for you as well! You'll need some help, support, and/or downtime afterwards (if that can be arranged).

Diagnosis of neurotypes

☐ Find out as much as you can about your child's neurotype, any provision for support for them, and the implications of getting a diagnosis, ideally *before* going ahead with it. It's great to have some awareness around what a diagnosis is, and what it means, both for you and your child. I'd highly recommend 'Not an Autism Mom's blog, if you haven't found it already.[68]

☐ Don't forget that, if you don't actively need any accommodations that would accompany a diagnosis (and you feel confident enough) it *is* an option to simply not get one! You can be autistic (or otherwise neurodivergent) without an official diagnosis.

☐ That's not to say that some children (and their parents) may not welcome a diagnosis, both because of the accommodations it might bring and finding that it explains why they are as they are. 'Ah, it's because I'm dyslexic!', and so on.

☐ I won't go into the steps to getting a diagnosis here as there are many sources available. But the WikiHow page 'How to Be Ready for an Autism Assessment' is helpful as a general guide (it's useful also for those who are going for other assessments, not just autism).[69]

☐ Be positive about your child's neurodivergence. Help them, if they're interested, find positive information and resources about neurodiversity, as this will lead to them feeling confident about it and about who they are.

☐ But if they show no interest, or are resistant to the idea, don't push it on them. Remember (especially for older kids) that they may have heard negative things about autism, 'special needs' and so on, for example, at school. Indeed, if your child gets a diagnosis but prefers people not to know about it, it's best to support them in this as much as you can.

☐ If your child is unhappy about being diagnosed but it's needed, you could (briefly!) explain the benefits that the process may bring to your child – if they're old enough to understand (and if not, you'll need to save that chat for a point in the future when they are old enough).

☐ Avoid using pathologizing language. Most autistic people aren't very happy about the use of the word 'disorder', so you can just imagine our feelings when people talk about it as an 'illness' or an 'epidemic' – and discuss 'cures' and so on.

☐ There's actually no need to use the terms 'high functioning' or 'low functioning'. These terms, besides being divisive and rather inhuman (when talking about humans as opposed to automobiles), can also be relatively unhelpful at times, as they overlook the fact that disability is context related. It's much more helpful to talk about 'support needs' or 'levels of support needed' instead.[70]

Traumatic stress

Some signs and symptoms of trauma are listed below. If you see your child exhibiting a range of these together, you can begin to suspect traumatic stress as the root cause.

Some of us parents may have already, at times, been puzzled to see (often unmistakable!) signs of traumatic stress in our neurodivergent children – but yet (we wonder, scratching our heads), there's nothing we can immediately spot that should be *causing* this sort of trauma.

In lots of parts of this book I've talked about sensitivity levels.[71] What may not cause *one* child trauma absolutely can and does cause another child to suffer it. And the same child could suffer trauma today from an experience that wouldn't have affected them last week, or last month (for example). There's unfortunately no handy manual of 'what does and doesn't cause children trauma'.

Signs to look out for

Here are some of the signs and symptoms commonly displayed by children when they're suffering, or have suffered, traumatic stress:

- outward character change (what has happened to my lovely, happy, kind son/daughter?)
- persistent controlling behaviours
- school avoidance/refusal (see Chapter 7, 'Learning and School')
- pervasive interest in death and suicide
- sudden, very strong, and often seemingly inexplicable reactions to triggers. Experiencing flashbacks
- sudden and frequent displays of strong anger and/or agitation – meltdowns
- chronic loss of appetite, or overeating
- major problems with focusing on projects, schoolwork, and conversation
- persistently disturbed sleeping habits, and nightmares
- chronic memory problems (e.g. extreme forgetfulness and short-term memory loss)
- problems with speaking/verbal expression (Broca's area – one of the speech centres in the brain – is affected)
- problems with interoception – that is, knowing/feeling what is going on in one's body (among other things, the Vagus Nerve is involved here, carrying motor and sensory information between the body and brain[72])
- problems with balance and movement, and bumping into things a lot without noticing (vestibular system is affected)
- persistent regressive behaviours (e.g. bed wetting, 'tantrums', consistently needing a parent or teddy at night again, panicking about being left alone)
- extreme acting out in social situations
- extreme avoidance of social situations

- shutdown/withdrawal in social situations (freeze reaction, when neither 'fight' nor 'flee' are available)
- persistent aggressive behaviours
- imitation of the traumatic event (look out for signs like mistreatment of pets or younger siblings as your child may be re-enacting what's happened to them), or enacting/showing it in their play or artwork
- excessive screaming or crying
- a tendency to startle easily, and to be very nervous or edgy a lot of the time
- inability to trust others or make friends
- self-blame, self-hate, excessive shame
- heightened fear of being separated from parent/caregiver
- fear of people who might remind them of the trauma
- persistent anxiety, fear, and avoidance
- chronic sadness and depression
- withdrawal and immobility overall (general listlessness, aimlessness, and marked tendency to 'freeze' when afraid)
- extreme and persistent lack of self-confidence, feeling a failure and worthless
- persistent digestive problems, stomach aches, and headaches.

What to do

If you're seeing signs of trauma in your child, you'll need to intervene as quickly and effectively as you can.

A child's ability to cope with the more challenging situations in their lives depends on:

- a healthy self-esteem and resilience
- avoiding situations that induce trauma (especially persistent/ repeated ones)
- a toolbox of good coping strategies (although note: coping

strategies should *not* need to be used systematically or longer-term).

A child who's in a chronic state of anxiety and/or panic due to on-going traumatic stress unfortunately doesn't have access to the re-sources listed above. Instead, the more and longer they suffer, a) the more severe their symptoms become, b) the less equipped they become to deal with further difficulties and challenges, and c) the longer their recovery period will need to be.[73]

To create an environment where healing can happen and resil-ience can grow, the first thing to do is to put in place (asap!) some proper downtime. This involves removing your child from potential sources of stress. Chapter 11, 'Emotions', coming up soon, will give the low-down on how to proceed after that.

TO SUM UP

This chapter has covered quite a few aspects of a child's health and wellbeing. All the time, our children are learning from us how to nurture and take care of their physical and mental selves. How to feel good (or better!).

And awareness about what it's like to feel good in your-self, and at home in your body, equips you to value that self – and look after that body – in ways that are truly beneficial long term.

CHAPTER 10

Physical Contact

When the soul feels trusting, and the senses aren't too over-whelmed.

Neurodivergent children can be quite diffident (or just plain confused!) around physical contact with other humans. Often, there are one or two things getting in the way of us finding it easy and enjoyable.

Being comfortable in your body

Being comfortable, and feeling at home in one's body, are prerequisites to having comfortable physical closeness with others.

For autistic people in particular, physical touch can simply be 'too much' on top of everything else the senses are being bludgeoned with in any given moment. I can't imagine that anyone whose tummy is churning from some overly complex food they've eaten, or whose skin is tortured with profoundly unpleasant sensations, or whose head is ringing with unbearable noise and chatter (and/

or who's overall feeling stressed, nervous and 'on-the-edge') really feels like being touched, kissed, or hugged, on top of that. Instead, they're already in a state of sensory 'red alert', in other words, very far from the state of happy relaxation in which we are most receptive to closer contact with others.

So, when we approach the topic of physical closeness and affection with our neurodivergent children, the first step is to make sure they're *physically comfortable*.

Physical comfort and safety

☐ Spend time in pleasant, comfortable environments. There are lots of ways the body and mind can relax, both when alone and in the company of others (more on this later, as well as in Chapter 2, 'At Home').

☐ Bear in mind that many (but not all) neurodivergent people prefer a firm touch as opposed to being stroked or lightly touched. In fact, many of us find the latter unbearable.

☐ Experiment with hair-brushing, head or neck massages, and/or back rubs and scratches (catering to your child's preferences – they'll quickly let you know if they like something or not). Both giving and receiving these can be really companionable and pleasurable.

☐ Let your child style and/or brush your hair, perhaps while you read to them or else in front of the TV. Especially if your child's a bit jumpy about physical touch, this is a great way to reassure them as, a) they are the proactive one, fully in control of the situation, and b) your attention is not focused on them. You may also get some great hairstyles out of it.

☐ Neurodivergent children probably won't enjoy being tickled. Indeed, most of us respond in horror even to the word, 'tickle'. However, for those few who do like it, make certain that the moment they say the word 'Stop' (or indicate they want you to stop) you instantly do so.

> To check I wasn't alone in my dislike of tickling, I ran a poll on neurodivergent Twitter and Mastodon on 11 December 2022, entitled 'Subject: Tickling'. I asked people if as children they had a) loved it, b) hated it, c) something else (comments). Out of 800 neurodivergent respondents, 86 per cent reported that as children they'd hated it.

☐ Instead of picking up children by their armpits (it's not very pleasant for them – in fact, it can hurt quite a lot), put one hand on the child's torso below one armpit, and the other one behind their knee/thigh on the opposite side (from the outside). You'll find the lift is less work for you into the bargain, as they've got more agency in it too.

Feeling comfortable with others

The other aspect about physical contact, predictably, is *trust*.

We need to feel truly safe around a person to want to snuggle up with them and be touched, hugged, and kissed by them – and hug, kiss, and snuggle them back! And we're generally unlikely to want to be physically close with people who we've found to be unpredictable, or who might, from one moment to the next, inflict things upon us that we find unpleasant, and that we have little choice about.

But rest assured, there are lots of ways to help our children avoid sensory overwhelm and feel safe enough to be more comfortable with physical contact and affection.

☐ Give your neurodivergent child unlimited access to gentle physical affection and contact (from the word 'go', i.e. from infancy).

☐ Note your child may not be comfortable with *unsolicited* shows of affection. Let them take the lead if you're uncertain or if they show any signs of discomfort.

☐ There will be times when your child won't want closeness (they may resist your embraces, go stiff or squirm when picked up or taken in an adult's arms, run away, or be rowdy when asked to be quiet and intimate). When this happens, the only thing we can do is remain philosophical.

Children must never be forced, coerced, or pressurized into making affectionate or loving gestures – with us or anyone else. If children, when unwilling or uncooperative in this regard, are pushed or persuaded into physical contact, they're actually being set up for future abuse.[74]

☐ Children might love physical contact with an animal, for example, a dog or cat, in moments when they don't want any other humans close to them. When this happens, as parents we need to be totally fine with it (maybe reminding ourselves firmly not to take it personally).

☐ Avoid physically restraining your child. Use every other means available, starting with respectful requests and brief explanations about things in carefully chosen moments. These will bear fruit, so be patient.

☐ Don't grab or yank, or force hold – nor allow anyone else to do so – outside situations that are *genuinely* life-threatening.

Physical restraint

If you find yourself with no choice but to use physical restraint for your child's own or others' safety (for example, if your child runs out onto a busy road), be aware that it's a very traumatic experience for your child (as well as for yourself) and that their trust in you may be quite badly damaged. Steps you can take to restore trust and connection are given in Chapter 11, 'Emotions'. And be kind to yourself too: it is a very hard job trying to weigh up complex risk scenarios and make split-second decisions to keep everyone safe.

- ☐ Give your child space when you see they're withdrawing. (More on this in Chapter 11, 'Emotions').
- ☐ Make it clear to your child that it's fine if they don't wish to accept or return gestures of affection from adults (whether it's from you or others). Support them in pre-empting and avoiding situations where they might feel pressure from others.
- ☐ If your child dislikes being touched and physically handled, try to talk beforehand to doctors and teachers (especially those teaching subjects like sports, dance, or gymnastics) to explain your child's needs and preferences around this.

TO SUM UP

Neurodivergent children need to be as physically comfortable as possible, and to feel safe (and to know they have a choice!) when it comes to situations involving contact with others. In this way, loving trust can grow.

Sometimes, it all gets to be a little too much...

CHAPTER 11

Emotions

Emotions, far from being 'silly' or 'irrational', are actually essential to our existence.

As a population, we rarely talk about emotions. And if we do, they tend to come low on the hierarchy and in fact are even denigrated ('you're being emotional', and so on). In answer to the question, 'How are you?', replying with a word such as 'happy', 'sad', or 'angry' (instead of with an explanation of what's happening in your life right now, or else just a simple 'fine') is something children may do, but we adults have learned not to.

Emotions, however, provide us with valuable information about what's happening in and around us. So rather than mastering them, denying them, suppressing them, and/or ridiculing and shaming people who openly experience them, perhaps we should be learning how to truly *feel* them and to use, and even share, this information. Maybe then we wouldn't go careering off in wrong directions all the time – which is what happens when we adamantly ignore our emotions in order to grasp at 'facts' and 'logic' (unaware that, if thoughts and ideas are the daisies, it's emotions that are the field).

Neurodivergent people are sensitive – both emotionally and to information coming through our senses (after all, the two are very closely linked). The *intrinsic* nature of neurodivergent people's sensitivity is often misunderstood – we cannot be cajoled, coerced, encouraged, or over-exposed out of it – even though we may learn to hide our distress and overwhelm, to 'mask',[75] or to find ways to make ourselves *feel* it all a bit less (some of which may become extremely problematic from a health perspective).

A lot of the time, therefore, we don't cognitively *know* how we feel. Imagine it as being rather like trying to listen to a soft voice when you're at a rock concert (one in which everyone's acting like it shouldn't be that difficult). We may, in desperation, 'act out' or else shut down/dissociate, often (especially in females) alongside habitual 'masking' and enduring in silence while pretending to be fine.

Communicating about emotions

Here are some tips around communicating about our emotions generally – whether verbally or not – and on ways to try to discern our children's emotional state.

- ☐ Mention how you feel sometimes. That may, especially if you're anything like me, involve first thinking about it! (There are more tips in the section below this one on ways to feel and understand one's own emotions.) This is easy enough when you're feeling great – 'I'm so happy!', 'I'm really excited because we're going on holiday!' – but when the feelings aren't so pleasant it gets harder. More in the following tips.
- ☐ Openly say to those around you if you're stressed or tired. This way, your children don't have to either wonder what's up (and if

you're angry with them) or feel a sense of stress or dread without knowing why.

☐ If you're annoyed with someone in your family – or rather, something that they did – try to address it immediately, or at least, when you've had time to calm down a bit and, if it helps, get some anger out (perhaps smashing up a few sticks in the woods or, if it's your thing, playing squash against a hardy opponent, or head-banging to some heavy metal music). Don't allow it to internalize. There's more in Chapter 6, 'Communication', about how to deal constructively with disagreements.

☐ Don't expect your child to be able to talk about their feelings, especially when they're upset.

☐ You could (if it feels right) mention to your child in a neutral moment, 'You know if there's ever anything that's bothering you, I'm here.' But make it clear you don't require any immediate reaction from them (or indeed, any reaction at all).

☐ Listen attentively whenever your child *does* communicate with you, taking care to neither correct them ('it can't be that bad') nor offer any fixes ('why don't you just...').

☐ Make it clear to your child that you consider it legitimate and perfectly normal to feel the way they do, in the circumstances.

☐ Carefully, in moments when your child seems receptive, and only if it feels natural and right (and while keeping a very open mind), you could try to help your child identify their own more difficult emotions. The following tips expand on this.

   – If your child is receptive, try asking them gently and flexibly what it feels like (also physically). Use simple questions, starting with yes/no ones. Stop talking if they ask you to, or if they're looking blank or defensive (observe their body language towards you, for example, if they're hunched, withdrawn, or turned away).

   – Avoid the 'why' question. Children (and indeed, most adults!)

may try obligingly to make some wild stabs at explaining *why* they're feeling a difficult emotion. But the truth is, until we've connected with ourselves compassionately, we won't have much chance of being able to answer the question very truthfully or helpfully.

Difficulties with identifying, understanding, and describing our emotions is a common feature of autism – and indeed of neurodivergence in general (sometimes known as 'alexithymia', loosely translating to 'no words for emotion'). Interestingly, however, we may sometimes feel *physical* symptoms in the place of *emotional* responses, for example, instead of nervousness, digestive problems; or instead of excitement, hives; or instead of fear, sudden drowsiness.

Feeling and expressing emotions

We need to first feel our emotions, allowing them in (so to speak) before we've got any hope of getting to the bottom of what they might mean.

☐ When your child shows strong emotions, focus on making them feel accepted and loved.
☐ A child might feel really scared and knocked off balance by their own strong emotions, so we need to let them know it's safe to express themselves (more on this in the 'Anger' section below).
☐ Be aware that neurodivergent children, despite not necessarily being able to fully express or understand their emotions, can be *extremely* sensitive to emotional undercurrents in the environment or from others around them.

It's no coincidence when a child becomes more demanding

and impossible in exactly the moment when everyone's getting stressed, or worried, or is hurrying.

☐ Outside of the more action-filled moments, have a think about any potential deeper reasons – and not just 'face value' ones – for your child's more explosive moments. (More on this, with practical tips, can be found in Chapter 4, 'Out and About', in the 'Meltdowns' section.)

'Radical Compassion'

☐ For a more systematic approach to feeling and coming to terms with your more difficult emotions (both for yourself and for your child), perhaps try out Tara Brach's technique, 'RAIN' as described in her book *Radical Compassion*.[76]

Tara Brach's 'RAIN' technique

If you're feeling a difficult, puzzling, or strong emotion, you can try these steps, taking plenty of time over them and stopping if you feel overwhelmed at any point:

R. Recognize what is going on for you. ('Ooh, look, I'm having a feeling!')

A. Allow the experience to be there, just as it is. ('Hello, feeling. It's okay...you can come in now')

I. Investigate with interest and care. (Here you take a look inside yourself, with curiosity. How does it feel in your body?[77])

N. Nurture yourself with compassion. (I say at this point, to myself or to another who I'm guiding through it, 'Here you just sort of hold and love yourself – as though you're someone you love very much indeed!')

But – before you start – please note that even forms of mindfulness as simple as the one I've described above can be complex for neurodivergent people and anyone who's suffered trauma. So please take great care, going slowly and observing closely for signs of distress (such as shaking or paleness) – and *never persist in exercises such as these if your child isn't 100 per cent happy to do it.*

Trauma and emotional healing

In the following sections I'll focus on emotional healing, including recovery from trauma. There's more information on traumatic stress itself – what it is, signs and symptoms to look out for, and its mid- to long-term effects – in Chapter 9, 'Health, Hygiene, and Fitness'.

Emotional withdrawal, or 'shut down'
They vary, but the main outward signs of emotional withdrawal are immobility or slow movement, paleness, dark shadows around the eyes, a body that looks floppy and boneless, an expressionless face, and eyes that may point sideways or downwards, or even be half closed. The child's body may rock back and forth. Other stims could include sucking on a thumb or lip or repeatedly pulling on the hair (these are attempts to soothe oneself).

Note: emotional withdrawal in children can be quite easily overlooked. Indeed, in a busy crowded setting, such as an institutional one, it may go entirely unnoticed!

☐ When you see your child withdrawing, don't make any demands or requests of them at all.
☐ Guide them to somewhere comfortable if you can; however, if they startle or indicate unwillingness, let them settle where they wish to.

☐ Make unobtrusive caring gestures – putting a drink or snack to hand or giving them a hot water bottle and/or a blanket if it's chilly. If they make any signs of physical withdrawal at your approach, simply put things down next to them.

☐ Verbally reassure your child you're there, and keep an eye out for whether they say/show that they need you to be physically close.

☐ Otherwise, stay nearby but unobtrusive. It can be extraordinarily reassuring having someone close by, but busy with their own things – such as cooking, knitting, studying, writing on a laptop, doing a crossword, or reading a book or magazine. But maybe stay off your smartphone; there can be something about that activity, which – if the other person present doesn't have a phone – can all too easily render you more absent than present (though it does depend what you're doing on it).

☐ A dog or cat can also be great for providing closeness.

☐ If you feel it might be well-received, you could offer to read to your child or accompany or help them in any preferred game or activity. (Note: activities that involve being emotionally present are best, so perhaps things like a puzzle, crafting, modelling, drawing, etc.)

☐ If they don't tense up, startle, or withdraw at your approach, after a while try sitting down next to them and see if they lean into you or not. Even if they don't, but your impression is that they like having you there, you could stay sitting near them but not directly focusing on them.

If they do lean into you, wanting a cuddle, give firm, reassuring pressure. You could offer a massage or head rub or similar if your child likes that. Basically, offer them just as much physical closeness (or as little!) as they wish for.

Autistic burnout

If stress is ongoing without let-up, and especially if your neurodivergent child habitually 'masks' (see below), then burnout may result.[78]

☐ Keep an eye out for general listlessness and fatigue in your child (see signs to look out for in the section above).

☐ Note any reduction in your child's capabilities – for example, inability to carry out habitual or daily tasks (whether cognitive or functional).

If you're seeing signs of burnout, it's time to prepare and settle in for a period of downtime and healing for your child. More about this in the next sections.

> 'Masking' is when we hide our neurodivergent traits and copy those around us (carefully observing people's reactions, all the time), so that we may appear more 'normal'.
>
> It's hard to imagine a) how much social pressure there is on us to do this (if we're humanly able), and b) how deeply it can harm and exhaust us – especially if 'masking' becomes persistent and habitual.
>
> For more information on autistic burnout, and on what you can do for your child, I'd recommend Helen Edgar's article 'Supporting Children through Autistic Burnout (Parent/Carer Guide)'.[79]

Note that, if your child has experienced trauma and/or has had a pronounced or prolonged withdrawal period (or autistic burnout), they may need a significant period – months, even – of downtime and safety before any stronger emotions, such as anger or grief, may start to come out.

Starting a healing process

Anger

Anger comes from pain and hurt, including, for example, loss, rejection, defencelessness, and being misunderstood. If anger gets habitually suppressed, it internalizes – manifesting over time in withdrawal, depression, shame, and destructive feelings towards oneself or the world.

Most of us are ill-equipped to deal with other people's anger, especially when those people are entirely dependent upon us as their caregiver. Indeed, we may be uncomfortably aware that a lot of our ways of reacting to a child's anger may not ultimately be very constructive – as they focus *only* on avoidance and suppression, while studiously ignoring the existence of reasonable factors that must have caused the anger in the first place.

In the following tips I'll go over some *different* ways of responding to a child's anger: ones that have a chance of a better outcome as they may get to, and even address, some of the root causes.

- ☐ Make it clear to your child that you're not going to ever judge them or stop loving them just because they're raging and rampaging.
- ☐ Listen to them (however they're expressing themselves), focusing fully on compassion and understanding what they're going through.
- ☐ Let them know you recognize all their feelings as 100 per cent legitimate.
- ☐ Don't react to anger with requests to 'calm down' or to apply self-control – or to 'think about nice things'. These methods at best postpone the problem, and, at worst, amplify it.

Anger is a defence mechanism that protects our emotional

selves against threats, comparable to how our immune system protects us from physical pathogens.[80]

If a child can't ever express their hurt and anger, and receives the message these feelings are misplaced, even shameful, they'll either a) direct their growing hurt and anger inwards instead, or b) feel ragingly angry with, and destructive against, the whole world. Or they may alternate between these two positions.

☐ Don't ask a child *why* they're angry. It's quite a confrontational question, and they probably won't be able to answer anyway (in the grip of strong emotions, our executive function – our ability to think and reason, and act accordingly – goes pretty much out of the window).

☐ Once a child has felt properly heard, understood, and safe, they'll gradually start showing and expressing to us what's up. We need to trust – both them and the process.

☐ Don't take it personally if your child's anger is directed at you – after all, you're their closest person.

Anger against the parent
My feeling is that even if you haven't personally done anything harmful (however, speaking as a parent, you may well have inadvertently done), your child may be feeling confused and betrayed that you haven't managed to protect them from other harmful things, without even being aware of it. Remember: this is never anything to do with blame. Not 'defending yourself' does not mean you are 'admitting blame'. However, it does mean you are taking responsibility – for the situation and for finding solutions – which is a different thing entirely.

☐ If your child's anger is directed at you, don't act defensively. Instead, find ways they can express the anger without hurting you

– examples could be a pillow fight, or them drawing a picture of you walking the plank into shark-infested seas with themselves as the Pirate Captain (the answer to that question you're thinking, by the way, is 'yes').

☐ Don't self-blame if you realize you have inadvertently caused harm, or allowed harm to happen. 'It's my fault' is as unhelpful as accepting no responsibility at all (and reinforces the idea that it's about fault and blame, as opposed to reaching understanding and finding good ways forward).

☐ Never, ever be tempted into offering 'positive reinforcements' for the non-expression of emotion. This (if it works) only postpones the problem and makes a child feel there's something wrong with them. It may also lead, over time, to dangerous self-soothing habits (especially if those rewards are substances that make you feel better, e.g. food).

☐ Let your child vent! Personally, I get quite enthusiastic in supporting my children in yelling or venting, as I find it can be fun, exhilarating, and bonding. But – don't take over. Remember this is their show.

☐ Start to explore creative ways in which the anger may be adequately but safely expressed. Some suggestions follow.

Ways to get anger out need to be things that a) work for the child, and b) are not harmful (either to themselves or others). Some examples:

- pillow fights and 'pillow rampages' (one person runs past getting 'shot at' with soft cushions, and then it's the other person's go)
- ripping up old sheets (one of my personal favourites)
- singing, rapping (even incoherently), playing drums or another musical instrument if your child is older and into that

- drawing pictures of how angry you are (yes, to my amazement, this can work!)
- dancing wildly round the living room to The Clash
- breaking sticks on the garden wall (wear gloves and protective glasses and keep your distance from one another, perhaps taking it in turns)
- stabbing half a watermelon murderously with a spoon
- punching a pillow or punching bag hanging from the ceiling
- running and yelling like crazy, in a field or on the beach
- flinging stones as far as you can into the sea or a lake.

And basically, anything else you can think of, that works and doesn't hurt.

☐ During all this, you've been left wondering about the deeper causes behind your child's anger and pain. As parents, at times like these we need to let our anxiety and impatience take a back seat, and simply trust the process (though there's no harm in quietly keeping a diary).

☐ However, if you feel it would help to have another brain on the job (and a trained one at that) you may want to turn to a therapist or counsellor for support and/or guidance.

☐ Bear in mind that large emotions of this kind tend to have both short-term reasons (commonly known as 'triggers') and deeper-flowing, longer-term reasons. It's useful to try to get to the bottom of both, as much as you can, without being either intrusive or obsessive about it.

☐ And it's very important we parents are willing to act, if necessary, on information coming out during the process.

☐ Finally, if you need to help your child through the sort of process I've described above, you *must* try to get some emotional support yourself. If not a partner, parent, sibling, or best friend, then try to see a therapist as the work I've described here is extremely draining – and may involve sleep deprivation, as well!

Sadness and grief

Some children go straight to grief, skipping anger – while others may alternate phases of each.

Here are some tips about what you could try doing if your child is sad or grief-stricken.

☐ Take *all* external pressures off your child.

☐ Provide them with silly amounts of safety and comfort.

☐ Offer unlimited access (on demand) to physical reassurance such as hugs, and, for smaller children, being carried in your arms.

☐ If they want you to hold them while they cry, do so. Do this tenderly but firmly (neurodivergent people tend to prefer a firmer touch to being stroked or lightly touched). There's no need to speak, although making reassuring noises can help.

☐ Never, ever show any signs of impatience or that you'd rather be doing something else.

☐ If your child doesn't want direct physical contact, remain present, but in the background quietly getting on with your own things; they'll benefit from benign, loving, non-demanding company. Animals can also be a great source of company and reassurance.

☐ Be ready if your child wants to talk about their feelings – and if they do, pay close attention and be fully present. Note that this does *not* necessarily mean staring them in the eyes or directing any laser-focused attention onto them – you could be for example, driving along together or zoning out in front of an old movie.

☐ If your child's having trouble expressing themselves (but clearly wants to), ask gentle, curious, 'clarifying' questions. If you're not sure if your child wants to be prompted, ask, 'Do you want me to ask you questions?' or even (if you think they may be having trouble knowing what they're feeling), 'Do you want me to try leading you through that "feeling feelings" exercise?' (see the section on 'Radical Compassion' above). Take your child's answer as definitive; do not apply persuasion.

☐ If your child seems happy for you to do so, you could suggest trying various things that might help them feel better (based on knowing them, observing, and past experience). There are some ideas in the following tips.

☐ If grief is mixed with any anger – or you suspect it's 'anger turned inwards' and/or shame (the clue is if the body is tensed in any way, or the jaw clenched) – you could suggest one or two of the 'getting anger out' exercises in your repertoire (see the section above on 'Anger').

Anger and grief

It's normal, in a period of healing, to pass between anger and grief. The anger is your psyche defending itself from harm endured (or being endured), and the grief is the acceptance and the 'catching up with yourself'.

☐ If it's just grief (the clue here is the body is relaxed, perhaps even sagging or crumpled), crying and being held is usually the first port of call. For just as long as your child needs to. Note: after a bout of weeping people may feel quite thirsty, so offer a glass of water.

☐ Some children may then benefit from physical attention such as a massage, having their hair brushed, or stroking or cuddling a favourite animal or teddy.

☐ Stimming can assist in releasing grief, so let your child use their preferred ones freely. Hand-flapping and rocking are common ones.

If your child's chosen stims are self-harmful ones, see the 'Stimming' section later in this chapter. Note that, in such cases, shame and/or anger may be at play, as well as grief.

- ☐ Once the storm's over, stay with your child. Provide closeness and warmth, just as much and for as long as they want you to.
- ☐ Offer your companionship, especially at night. Your child may want to chat with you, listen to music, or have stories or talking books together – and snuggle up together.

My children, after feeling unhappy, always wanted to have my old teddy (an owl) tell them stories. To this day she still occasionally does so. It's incredible the number of adventures that old owl has had! The kids intervene with any suggestions – in fact, many of the inventions featuring in the 'Owlie' stories are theirs.

- ☐ Over time, observe whatever small things or circumstances appear to make your child feel better through the day (look for an open, uplifted face and shining, engaged eyes), and what seems to make them worse (look for downcast eyes and a pale anxious face, hunched shoulders, and/or jitteriness).
- ☐ Make a list for yourself, preferably when your child isn't present. Try to focus on doing the things that make your child feel good, avoiding the bad things, until they're feeling resilient enough to be more adventurous again.
- ☐ Don't lose sight of the bigger picture. I've found keeping a diary helps, as it reassures me that things *are* changing, albeit gradually and with setbacks here and there (sometimes quite big ones!).
- ☐ But if you feel you're not managing to deal with and alleviate your child's anger or grief, seek professional help from a therapist. Do not feel you've failed. It's not you – this is *hard!* Especially if you're doing it all alone and have no choice but to keep other shows on the road too (which, let's face it, is usually the scenario).

If your child has suicidal thoughts or self-harms

I've put these two topics together, not because the situations are the same, but because the sentiments and motivations behind them are likely to be quite similar.

The emotions at play here are anger, grief, turmoil, despair, emptiness, or a combination of these. And the events and drivers that have led to these could include things like frustration, overwhelm, shame, and disillusionment. These huge and difficult emotions, in the absence of any outlet or perceived alternative, have now been turned inwards upon the self.

Note: if you feel any suicide attempt is imminent, or if the results of self-harm are serious and/or might need medical treatment, turn immediately to your local services, starting with your GP and/or a therapist (or the nearest hospital, if there are injuries).

☐ Take all external pressures off your child (even if this means taking time off work or making other arrangements).

☐ Make your child's physical environment as comforting and pleasant as you can. Provide their favourite food, their stim toys, gentle lighting, soft towels, some lavender, and so on.

☐ Make sure it's a pleasant temperature for them. If they're in bed, and it's cold in the room, bring them a fluffy hot water bottle (okay, it doesn't *have* to be fluffy!). If it's hot, open a window or provide a fan.

☐ Make sure there's fresh, cool drinking water to hand.

☐ Provide lots of contact and affection, if wanted. And let any pet stay with them, if that's what the child wants.

☐ Note: your physical presence, and especially touch/holding, is best when accompanied with your real 'presence' – it's better *not* to lie or sit there frantically thinking about your emails or tomorrow's 'to-do' list, or to be on your smartphone.

☐ Instead, if, say, you're lying with your child in your arms, try to focus on your breathing – and (if you're a pro at this!) you could even try meditating a loving mantra to your child, or just think over some loving, wonderful times you've had together.

Self-harm
This might happen in situations of great emotional pain and of powerlessness.
The reasons behind it are usually that:

- Physical pain can feel more manageable than huge emotional pain.
- Extreme emotional pain can cause numbness. Physical pain may 'remind you you're alive'.

Note: Toxic shame (self-hate or self-contempt coming out of internalized hurt and anger) and self-harm are closely linked. This shame has generally come from someone else, or others, or human society at large having inflicted intolerable pain upon you – often, in the case of neurodivergent people, because of having been brought (however gently!) to understand that you are faulty.[81]

☐ Don't display shock, disbelief, or open worry at *anything* your child reveals to you, as they'll probably feel even worse for inflicting this on you, and/or that there's something wrong with them.
☐ If your child shows signs of wanting to communicate about their feelings, be receptive. There's more on this in the 'Communicating about emotions' section above.
☐ Don't be tempted into being 'positive'. Statements like, 'But you have so much to live for!' or, 'It'll get better, you'll see,' can be astonishingly unhelpful in these situations.

When another person is feeling strong emotions, it's best to allow them to be wherever they're at, accept it, and even join them there (for example in your thought, speech, or imagination). In fact, the meaning of the word 'compassion' is 'suffering with'.

When a person feels less alone, and less badgered to be 'different' from how they currently are, they'll feel very reassured.

I see it a bit like trying to get a frightened kitten to come out from behind a piece of furniture. The more you cajole, call, implore, and tell them, 'It's fine out here!', the further in they go and the more unreachable they become. If, on the other hand, you lie down nearby and quietly read a book or go to sleep, the next thing you know they're curled up on top of you.

- ☐ Parallel play can feel very reassuring to a child who's 'on the edge'. A friend described to me how, when she was not in a very good shape, her auntie brought around a jigsaw puzzle, which they quietly did different parts of together.
- ☐ The presence of an animal can also be grounding and therapeutic (more on pets in Chapter 2, 'At Home').
- ☐ Spending time in nature, if possible, has healing powers too (more in Chapter 4, 'Out and About').
- ☐ In all of this, never show any signs of impatience. Your child mustn't *ever* receive the message that looking after them is inconvenient (even if it is, from a worldly perspective!).
- ☐ Come to terms with the fact some lifestyle changes are probably going to be necessary (while trying not to get freaked out at this thought – after all, healing first!).

More on ways to embark on a healing process can be found in the 'Anger' and 'Sadness and grief' sections above.

The healing process – mid- to long-term

☐ When starting to return to daily routines, do it gradually, following your child's lead on how much they can manage (and observing them closely at every step).

☐ Be aware that before having any hope of returning to daily life, any specific areas of tension and anxiety for your child will need to be alleviated or even eliminated, alongside focusing on downtime and pleasant activities.

☐ Keep things as physically comfortable and pleasant for your child as you can (more in Chapter 2, 'At Home').

☐ Introduce regular habits and rituals your child enjoys[82] (e.g. an episode or two of a favourite TV series every evening, or reading aloud a chapter of a story each night).

☐ Keep a goodly amount of your child's 'safe foods' in the house.

☐ Let your child lie on the sofa in your communal area when they need to rest while you get on with your daily tasks (e.g. setting up the TV there for them to watch).

☐ If your child's up for it, do some outings (perhaps every day or every couple of days), starting small.

☐ If you have a garden or terrace sit outside or even, for example, have a barbecue or plant some seeds in pots. Or you could take mini outings to the park, having a stroll and an ice cream or some salty chips.

☐ Don't panic if there are relapses. This is normal in the healing process.[83] Simply retreat to previous steps (lots of patience and faith are required).

☐ Don't put deadlines or limits on periods of healing. Children are more likely to bounce back (and faster!) when we *genuinely* don't impose any time restrictions on them.

☐ Seek emotional help and support for yourself, if possible; you'll need it. Especially helpful could be someone who has professional training and can be spoken with in confidentiality, such as a counsellor.

Stimming – emotional self-regulation

'Stimming' is short for 'self-stimulatory behaviour' and refers to habits or behaviours (often repetitive) whose purpose is to self-regulate and self-soothe. Stimming is usually an important feature of neurodivergent people's lives. We use it for emotional and sensory self-regulation, and it's often involuntary (or even, at times, completely unconscious!).

We may stim in anything from very happy, creative, or 'connected' moments, to moments of extreme distress, fear, or anxiety.

Stimming can include movements of the body, face, or hands – such as hand-flapping, rocking, jumping, spinning, or twirling, head-banging, and more complex body motions. It can involve objects or toys – perhaps touching, flicking, twirling, or squashing them, or simply repeatedly feeling things that have certain textures. Or it can be visual, for example looking at a spinning light or fan. Stims could be verbal ones involving repeating certain words or sounds; this is known as 'echolalia'. Put it this way, if there was a dictionary of stims, it would be a very large one!

☐ Let your child stim freely, without looking upon it in any way negatively or reprovingly.

☐ If there are situations where your child's stimming is attracting negative attention (e.g. bullying at school) you could try to provide them with alternatives, such as a stim toy or chewable necklace. But beware here, as habitual masking (which includes supressing our stims) can be extremely bad for the health. See 'Autistic burnout' earlier in this chapter.

Self-harmful stims

Some stims are less benign. These could be skin-picking, head-hitting, hair-pulling, biting or slapping oneself, or nail-biting – among many other things. The following are some strategies to apply if your child has any self-harmful stims.

Pre-emptive measures

Depending on the stim, there may be some preventative actions that can be taken.

☐ The presence of an animal such as a cat or dog, to play with and stroke, can calm a child and divert their attention.

☐ For skin-picking or nail-biting, a child could wear long-sleeved T-shirts and/or always have short nails.

☐ For skin-picking, try putting face-mask cream or mud onto the child's face or arms, so they can pick that off instead.

☐ Have stim-toys handy – whether spinners, squidgies, dimple toys, or whatever the child likes best.

☐ For biting or chewing stims, try using 'chewellery'. This refers to chewable, wearable objects such as necklaces, pendants, and bracelets.

Basically, use any solutions you can think of that are respectful, helpful, and non-intrusive – and that the child is happy with.

What to do in the moment

☐ When a child starts a self-harmful stim, stay present, stay calm, and stay loving.

☐ Avoid any direct physical interventions as these can be traumatic for the child.

☐ But stay quite close – if possible – and make it clear that you're available for any hugs, hand-holding, massages, or reassurance (but only if it's desired).

☐ Note that direct focus, for example people looking at the child or talking about them, can be less than helpful. Ask others to leave the space if that's an option; if not, request them to turn their attention elsewhere.

☐ Now, modify the environment a) in ways that permit your child to continue to stim but less harmfully, and b) making everything overall less overwhelming/stressful for them. Examples are given in the next tips.

☐ Make the lighting lower, if possible.

☐ Place mats along the wall or on the floor if your child is hitting their head on it. Lay down some pillows and cushions on the ground around them, or a thick rug or more mats.

☐ If your child is biting themselves, hand them other things to bite on.

☐ Offer your child something reassuring to hold or feel, perhaps a stress or fidget toy – or, if they're unapproachable, just place it within reach.

☐ If your child enjoys music, try putting on some soothing tunes for them.

☐ And, besides limiting damage in ways that are respectful and unintrusive, simply be unconditionally available to your child as soon as they may feel they need you (ways to help with anger and grief are in the sections above).

Mid-term

☐ It's best not to remove or forbid a child's favourite stim or make them feel there's censure and disapproval around it (as that stim may well get replaced by another, perhaps even less benign, one).

☐ Instead, try introducing new stims alongside it, experimenting with different things.

☐ If your child's amenable, in calmer moments try talking with them about what works for them and what doesn't.

☐ Avoid telling your child you're worried about them, or overall giving them the message there's something wrong with them. If you do (even inadvertently), they'll feel more shame and pressure – which could lead to even more self-harmful stims than otherwise.

☐ Start a 'quiet investigation' about what's happening overall for your child, noting things down and trying to spot any patterns.

Longer-term

It's good to look at the bigger picture, to try to gain some perspective on *why* harmful stims are being used – and in which situations.

Take notes on a) what was happening before a harmful stim began, b) the environment, and c) your child's overall wellbeing at that time, or signs of pre-existing stress. For example:

- What's the lighting like and are there any annoying, persistent, or loud noises?
- Might the child be in any physical discomfort (hot, cold, sore tummy, and so on)?
- In the run-up to this, have they attracted any unwanted attention, or been the centre of attention, or heard people talking about them negatively?
- Have they been the witness or recipient of any unfairnesses or illogic, for example, 'different rules for different people'?
- Have they had any of their wishes or preferences disregarded, or their things moved or changed without their consent, or their routines altered?

Painful stims can be a child's attempt to manage and mitigate emotional or sensory pain. A pain you can control is preferable to one you can't.

> To quote an autistic person: 'For me, self-harming stims and behaviours are autistic, OCD, and trauma related. Which means it's tied to overstimulation, inner and outer anxiety, shame, and flight/flight lack of control.'

☐ Once you've identified triggers for your child's self-harmful stims, you can begin to pre-empt and avoid those situations.

☐ Alongside this, reduce pressures overall on your child. This can best be done in a holistic manner, focusing on increasing their feelings of sensory comfort and emotional safety, and reducing anxiety levels.

> In periods when your child is feeling more overwhelmed and stressed than usual, their stimming may become more pronounced, and harmless stims may evolve into more harmful ones.

On emotional punishment

In our society, we often use tools such as ostracism, disapproval, and ridicule (sometimes with an almost-imperceptibly light 'it wasn't me' sort of a touch) to 'teach' people things. And unfortunately – even if we don't in principle think this is a good idea – we may do it anyway, completely unawares.

With neurodivergent children, things can go spectacularly wrong when we use these techniques. They'll have no clue what's happening, or why, and will feel less and less safe on this shifting, nonsensical, painful ground – so they'll either act up or withdraw.

The following are some tips that might prevent this from happening.

☐ Be straight and open with your child, both with any requests of them and about your own feelings. There are more specifics about this in the following tips.

☐ Don't poke fun at your children (no, not even affectionately!) or be disapproving when they are exuberant, impassioned, or wildly enthusiastic. Roll with it. Be enthusiastic too!

☐ Don't act hurt or annoyed without giving your children the reasons you're acting that way. Instead, try saying how you feel: 'I'm really tired' or 'I get stressed and irritable when we have to hurry.'

☐ Don't hold grudges or give off an aura of disapproval or disappointment.

Lots more tips on encouraging open, honest, and loving connection are given in Chapter 5, 'Friendship', while tips on how to foster good communication channels with your child, and how to deal with more complex situations involving your interactions, can be found in Chapter 6, 'Communication'. There are also some tips on expressing your own feelings in the 'Communicating about emotions' section earlier in this chapter.

On needing control – and feeling out of control

Some neurodivergent children seem to have an overriding desire or need to control their external environment.

My own theory is that the habits, rituals, and everyday routines that humans would truly thrive within would be of the 'home-grown' variety and very family and community oriented. Most of our habits, routines, and rituals would revolve around people and places we'd know well and already feel relatively comfortable with. We'd perhaps be kinder to one another and not compete so much – collaborating instead. There'd be fewer gaps to fall through and fewer hoops to jump through – logistically and emotionally. As it is, however, hierarchically governed, top-down, medium-to-large institutions and networks make up most of our lives. Our current setup means that our daily lives often do not feel very 'human-sized'. And, I believe, people don't generally feel intrinsically safe within it; it feels sometimes like it wasn't made for real, warm, sensitive, contact-craving, air-breathing humans.

Since we can't change things structurally, however, I feel all we can do, as parents, is try to both recognize and mitigate the effects this situation has on our children. And especially our neurodivergent ones, as they're exceptionally sensitive.

The best antidote is having a foundation of trust – in oneself, in others, and in the universe. And this is something that *can* be nurtured by a child's carers.

We can help our children – as much as is in our power – to form secure, loving, trusting connections, both within the family and outside it (more tips on how to nurture these sorts of connections in Chapter 5, 'Friendship' and Chapter 6, 'Communication'); nurture their sense of personal stability and self-esteem (more on this in Chapter 2, 'At Home' and Chapter 3, 'Downtime and Hobbies'); and help them feel at home – both in their bodies and in the world (more in Chapter 9, 'Health, Hygiene, and Fitness' and Chapter 4, 'Out and About').

Note: practical tips on routines and fostering a reasonable flexibility in our children can be found in Chapter 2, 'At Home', under 'Routines, predictability and inflexibility'.

TO SUM UP

This chapter has focused heavily on the harder aspects of emotional wellbeing. The rest of the book (in chapters such as, 'At Home', 'Out and About', 'Friendship', and so on) covers a lot of ground about being happy and fulfilled, both in ourselves and with one another.

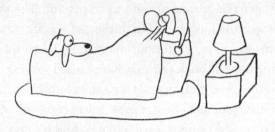

CHAPTER 12

Bedtime

O bed! O bed! delicious bed!
That heaven upon earth to the weary head.
Thomas Hood, 1840

Parents are usually much keener on the idea of bedtime than children are. And neurodivergent children can have *particular* issues around sleeping and bedtime. The factors at play here are usually overstimulation, high levels of vigilance/anxiety,[84] and (on occasion) physical discomfort such as digestive problems.

Getting good sleep is important for a person's self-regulation, resilience, and wellbeing. This means that nurturing happy and healthy sleeping in our child is a priority, both for their wellbeing and for ours! So, we need to make them feel as safe and as comfortable as we can.

We humans are biologically predisposed for sleeping near one another. For hundreds of thousands of years, we'd sleep close together. Hearing others breathing, feeling the presence of them near us, would have told us all was well with the world. All this, hard as we may try, can't be turned around in an instant. The thing is, as individuals we're no longer used to this sort of regular close physical contact – for example, within our own family when we ourselves were growing up. Although this may have caused varying degrees of suffering at the time, it means that we adults (especially, perhaps, if we're neurodivergent ourselves) aren't likely to cope well with having our children around us both night and day. And it's no small detail that our situation is *not* a communal one, as in such a situation we would never be left as the lone, sole carers of our children, night and day. This renders the situation untenable, for the simple reason that the main carer never gets any downtime at all (or vanishingly rarely). So, our night-times may start to look incredibly precious to us.

I hope this goes some way to explaining why, in this chapter, I may sometimes sound like I'm contradicting myself. On the one hand I'm saying, 'reassure your child' and 'always be there when they need you', and on the other I'm telling you that you *do* need time off and away from your children, and I'm giving tips on how that goal may be (albeit gradually) achieved. Basically, my take is to try to cover as many ways I can think of that your child can feel so *very* safe, comfortable, and loved that there will be movement towards self-regulation as rapidly as can be hoped.

Indeed, the aim – besides the obvious one of having a happy and healthy child – is towards getting night-times back for yourself. At least sometimes.

Preparing for bed and sleep

☐ Some parents find it helps to take a few moments for themselves, to transition from 'daytime' mode to more relaxed 'evening' mode – before starting the evening and bedtime routine.

☐ Having a regular routine that works for your family (perhaps keeping an eye on the clock, at first, if things tend to slip) really, really helps. This will depend on you and your family, of course, but some things that may be included are given in the following tips.

☐ Don't have dinner too late.

☐ Maybe read a bedtime story to your children (or a chapter or two of a bigger book, for older children), as this is quite a companionable and calming activity and, again, taps into an ancient tradition among humans: telling one another stories. One strategy is to take a break between chapters for changing into pyjamas, brushing teeth, and so on. If you're watching a film, you could pause it and have an 'interval' for this purpose.

☐ Get ready for bed (so in pyjamas, teeth brushed) early enough so everyone's still perky. If you wait too long, people get over-tired and crotchety (and that includes the parents!).

☐ Include a non-sweet snack at some point. If your kids tend to get hungry last thing, it's better to do this, for example, an hour before bed than to risk having your child get into bed, put the light off, then suddenly announce, 'I'm hungry'. Plain-ish snacks are best at this point – such as oatcakes or rice cakes, or some low-sugar cereal.

☐ Some kids need a last 'sensory-seeking' spurt before bedtime. This could include listening to a favourite track, dancing, or playing with their fidget toys. If this applies to your child, incorporate it into the bedtime routine.

☐ Some find that a warm bath can really soothe, calm, and relax them towards bedtime, perhaps with some soothing tunes as well.

☐ Massage and/or yoga exercises can be relaxing. (Note: massage can also really help soothe a child who's suffering any physical discomfort, such as tummy ache or cramps.)

The sleeping environment

☐ Try not to keep too much clutter in bedrooms – or keep belongings and toys in a way that you and/or your child can put things away easily in cupboards or boxes.

☐ Have different options for lighting in the bedroom – the 'bedtime' lighting being much lower, warmer lighting (such as a bedside lamp).

☐ Fluffy hot water bottles shaped like animals are great to snuggle with.

☐ Some children love projector lights that change colour and/or have shapes that move across the walls and ceiling. Others may love 'glow-stars' – luminescent stars that 'charge up' when the lights are on to then glow in the dark later.

☐ Look into using pressure for reassurance. Many neurodivergent people swear by weighted blankets. Some may find that (thinking of a specific friend) a largeish or weighted toy can be reassuring on the chest (hers was a furry cat – and now she has a real one!). There are also many weighted pillows and shaped cushions available.

☐ Natural, familiar smells/scents can help a child feel safe and relaxed at bedtime. Some oils and scents are known to assist in relaxation and sleep, such as lavender (but keep an eye on allergies when trying anything new!).

☐ A cool-temperature room – while the bed itself is warm and cosy – and a little fresh air for oxygen (see if it's possible to leave a window on 'air trickle') can help with both falling asleep and sleeping deeply.

☐ Try not to have screens or devices in the bedrooms (at least, not for younger kids). Bedrooms, ideally, should be areas of peace – both of environment and of mind. If your child has a gaming device or computer setup, try to have this somewhere besides their bedroom. It could, for example, be in the corner of a communal area such as a living room or living/kitchen area.

☐ Getting out in the fresh air for a bit of exercise every day can make a big difference to how well children sleep at night.

Falling asleep

Sleep is a vulnerable state. If we don't feel intrinsically trusting and relaxed, it's easy to see why we would not voluntarily give ourselves up to it. Safety and reassurance are of the essence here.

☐ Place a comfy armchair next to your child's bed, where you can sit for a while when they feel insecure or have a nightmare (it should be very comfy and equipped with a warm blanket).

☐ Try singing to your children while they fall asleep. Babies and small children can find this really soothing (and it doesn't matter in the least if you're not in tune!).

☐ Stay awake till your child has fallen asleep. I know this can be hard, but it's important – as otherwise children's hypervigilance is likely to become worse as they know you may not 'stay with them'. This means they may take longer and longer to fall asleep, which means you're more and more likely to fall asleep yourself (i.e. it's a vicious circle).

☐ Even after you think your child is fast asleep, count to a hundred in your head before daring to stand up (in my experience, this gives a higher successful-exodus rate).

☐ Some children like some soothing music or white noise while they fall asleep.

☐ Others might like a talking book while dropping off to sleep (and they may become attached to certain favourites).

☐ For those who've experienced such difficulty sleeping that they've developed a real fear around it, some families find that a period of using melatonin can help, as prescribed by a doctor (see the section on 'Medication' in Chapter 9, 'Health, Hygiene, and Fitness', for more on medications in general).

☐ When your child is learning to sleep – and to fall asleep – alone, tell them you'll come back in a bit to 'check on them' and 'tuck them in'. And don't forget to do so! Even if they are usually asleep when you come. Note: we've been through phases where I had to come and 'tuck someone in' five or six times before they'd succumb to sleep. But, I figured, it was important, as this way they learned I *would* come back (i.e. I was still present and awake, even if I wasn't in the room with them).

☐ Bear in mind, if it's all feeling frustrating and repetitive, that it's a phase. They will, eventually, grow out of it. It's about being conditioned into feeling safe. Your child is learning they're not alone and everything's all right with the world – it's safe to fall asleep.

☐ With older children who've learned to sleep alone, when saying 'goodnight' and leaving the room, ask them if they want their door open, closed, or ajar. And add, 'And you know where to find me if you need me.'

Through the night

Children who don't have the option to be close to someone in the night, should they feel the need, may get very fearful, distressed, and lonely, especially sensitive children who are prone to anxiety. They may start to lose their trust in people (as they aren't there in their darkest moments) and to dissociate and even withdraw away from others – because it's too painful to admit, even to yourself, that you *need* them. I probably don't need to say that I don't think this is the best way to condition a young human.

Some ideas for providing enough reassurance, contact, and

company for your child through the night, hopefully without totally wiping yourself out in the process, can be found below.

☐ When your child is little, it's best if they have the option of sleeping in the same room as you – whether that's in their room or yours (perhaps you can creep away during the hours the child sleeps, if you need time to yourself or with your partner).

☐ Later, siblings may often prefer to sleep in the same room as one another, but make sure it's what everyone wants! Also ensure there's an option for one or the other to sleep with you, or elsewhere, if they need to.

☐ Have as little distance as possible between your bedroom and your children's, and sleep with the doors between you open. It's important you're able to hear if your child wakes up and needs you as they may be too scared to come to you by themselves. Note: having additional fire alarms, in strategic points, can help those who worry about the added fire hazard of leaving doors open at night.

☐ Have nightlights in the corridor and/or bedrooms.

☐ Having a dog or cat can really help with providing a child with company at night-times – perhaps the dog's bed could be in the corner of your child's bedroom. Even the company of a hamster or tortoise (in their cage/terrarium) can make a big difference for a child (although note, hamsters are nocturnal and can make quite a lot of noise at night).

☐ Tell your child they need never be anxious, lonely, or frightened on their own at night and that you *much* prefer they wake you up than ever to feel like that.

☐ If they do wake you up in the night, don't show *any* annoyance or impatience, nor suggest – or even hint! – to them that they'd have been fine on their own or that they shouldn't have woken you. (I know it can be hard to do this. Especially if you've got work the next day.) Instead, be warm, welcoming, and loving. And assume that if they came, or called, it's because they need you.

☐ Trust that the more your child feels supported at night and knows there's somewhere to turn if they ever feel lonely or frightened, the less they'll need to avail themselves of the opportunity.

TO SUM UP

We are now at the end of the bedtime chapter – and indeed, the end of the book. I hope some of the tips may have been helpful to you. And just to emphasize once again: the tips I've given aren't ever intended as prescriptive or as 'rules' to follow. There are lots of things that may work for some but really wouldn't work for others – everyone's situation is unique!

And finally

A word for parents

Being a parent is such an enormous task that it's hard to know where to begin with this, but I felt I just had to add that I'm well aware of the difficulties in giving our children the kind of care and support we might wish them to have.

If your child is autistic or otherwise neurodivergent – well, this can be the point where we enter the realms of the unbelievable in how difficult it can become. But perhaps it's also the point at which many of us begin to question and change ourselves and 'how things are done', hopefully leading the way to real change for the better.

This is the reality: each of us is working mainly in isolation. Only the luckiest of families can manage on one income or receive welfare support that's sufficient to survive on, while those who also have to work for money will find themselves not just on night duty with the kids but cleaning the bathroom at midnight or sorting the toy cupboard before dawn (on no extra pay and with no recognition). How anyone can be patient and loving in such circumstances beats me!

But even for those who have support financially, we live in a world that does not value parenting or homemaking as an occupation, either full or part time, and in which (when we do dedicate time to them) we're labouring away unseen and unrecognized in our little individual pods. I don't find any of this an ideal arrangement as there is usually no adult company, no friendly sharing of work among equals, and no moment of freedom from responsibility and no real time off – not even at night.

Besides isolation and lack of recognition, another problem for parents is that even if you do spend a lot of time with other adults, how many of those are your real 'clan'? Because of the way the world currently works, we can't automatically trust everyone around us. Many of us – more than can be imagined, I think (since we're usually unaware of it) – have had our own experiences that can easily result in us behaving cruelly, neglectfully, or inappropriately to others, including children.

It seems to me that what we're all suffering from, to varying degrees, is a deficit of real connection with ourselves, with others, and with a well-functioning and kindly community – as well as lack of free time and time spent quietly by ourselves and/or in nature.

All I can say is that in such circumstances it's very difficult to raise our children with all the joy and humanity we would wish them to experience now, and in their future lives. So, if you manage to achieve it even *just a little* – and with however many lapses and confusions along the way – then you're not only contributing to your child's happiness and future, but to everyone's!

You are actively contributing to the creation of a more humane and beautiful world for us all.

Here's to you, parent, and miracle-worker!

Some books

These are a few of the titles I've read recently that I've found incredibly relevant, interesting, and useful. I'm listing them here in case they may also be helpful to you.

Ballou, Emily Paige et al. *Sincerely, Your Autistic Child: What People on the Autism Spectrum Wish Their Parents Knew About Growing Up, Acceptance, and Identity.* Autistic Women and Nonbinary Network. Beacon Press; 2021.

Beardon, Luke. *Avoiding Anxiety in Autistic Children: A Guide for Autistic Wellbeing.* Sheldon Press; 2021.

Delahoke, Mona. *Beyond Behaviors: Using Brain Science and Compassion to Understand and Solve Children's Behavioral Challenges.* PESI Publishing; 2019.

Faber, Adele and Mazlish, Elaine. *How to Talk So Kids Will Listen and Listen So Kids Will Talk.* Piccadilly Press; 2017.

Fisher, Dr Naomi. *Changing Our Minds: How Children Can Take Control of Their Own Learning*. Robinson; 2022.

Greene, Ross W. *Raising Human Beings: Creating a Collaborative Partnership with Your Child*. Scribner; 2017.

Holt, John. *How Children Learn (Classics in Child Development)*. Da Capo Lifelong Books; 1995.

Kohn, Alfie. *Unconditional Parenting: Moving from Rewards and Punishments to Love and Reason*. Atria Books; 2006.

Liedloff, Jean. *The Continuum Concept: In Search of Happiness Lost (Classics in Human Development)*. Da Capo Press; 1986.

Mavir, Heidi. *Your Child Is Not Broken: Parent Your Neurodivergent Child Without Losing Your Marbles*. Bluebird; 2024.

Miller, Alice. *The Drama of Being a Child*. Virago; 1995.

Neufeld, Gordon and Maté, Gabor. *Hold On to Your Kids: Why Parents Need to Matter More Than Peers*. Ballantine Books; 2006.

Walker, Nick. *Neuroqueer Heresies: Notes on the Neurodiversity Paradigm, Autistic Empowerment, and Postnormal Possibilities*. Autonomous Press; 2021.

Wassell, Cathy. *Nurturing Your Autistic Young Person: A Parent's Handbook to Supporting Newly Diagnosed Teens and Pre-teens*. Jessica Kingsley Publishers; 2022.

Endnotes

1   Terra Vance. *On Rejection Sensitive Dysphoria, Codependency, & Identity.* NeuroClastic. 2 October, 2022. https://neuroclastic.com/on-rejection-sensitive-dysphoria-codependency-identity-how-to-get-out-from-behind-the-masks

2   Laura Dattaro. *Largest study to date confirms overlap between autism and gender diversity.* 14 September, 2020. www.spectrumnews.org/news/largest-study-to-date-confirms-overlap-between-autism-and-gender-diversity

3   Lisa Legault. *Intrinsic and Extrinsic Motivation.* Clarkson University, November 2016. www.researchgate.net/publication/311692691_Intrinsic_and_Extrinsic_Motivation

4   Mona Delahooke. *Beyond Behaviors: Using Brain Science and Compassion to Understand and Solve Children's Behavioral Challenges.* PESI Publishing; 1st edition, 2019.

5   Natalie Engelbrecht and Eva Silvertant. *The Autistic Experience of Shut-Down.* Embrace Autism. 3 May, 2021. https://embrace-autism.com/the-autistic-experience-of-overwhelm

6 Kalina Jones. *'Control Issues' and Autistics: Understanding & Navigating a Basic Autistic Needs.* 1 October, 2021. https://neuroclastic.com/control-issues-and-autistics-understanding-navigating-a-basic-autistic-needs

7 Samuel Hunley. *Executive Functioning and How It Relates to Anxiety.* 6 October, 2023. www.anxiety.org/what-is-executive-functioning-and-how-does-it-relate-to-anxiety

8 Sarah MacLaughlin. *What Parents Need To Know About Counterwill.* 22 July, 2016. https://sarahmaclaughlin.com/what-parents-need-to-know-about-counterwill-and-a-book-review

9 Alfie Kohn. *Punished by Rewards: The Trouble with Gold Stars, Incentive Plans, A's, Praise, and Other Bribes.* Houghton Mifflin; 2018. www.alfiekohn.org/punished-rewards

10 Sujan Vijayraj Shadrak. *How Playing an Instrument Affects Your Brain* (video) 17 November, 2020. www.brainfacts.org/neuroscience-in-society/the-arts-and-the-brain/2020/how-playing-an-instrument-affects-your-brain-111720

11 Carly Cassella. *Study Shows the Effect Petting Your Dog or Cat Has on Stress Level.* Science Alert, 18 July 2019. www.sciencealert.com/petting-a-cat-or-dog-for-just-ten-minutes-can-lower-your-stress-hormones-study-finds

12 National Disability Insurance Agency of Australia (NDIA). *Animal-assisted interventions.* 5 July, 2021. www.ndis.gov.au/about-us/research-and-evaluation/early-childhood-interventions-research/autism-crc-early-intervention-report/animal-assisted-interventions

13 The Gentle Barn (USA): www.gentlebarn.org/children; Dogs for Autism' (UK): https://dogsforautism.org.uk

14 Pete Wharmby. *What I Want to Talk About: How Autistic Special Interests Shape a Life.* Jessica Kingsley Publishers; 2022.

15 Niza Stiglic and Russell M. Viner. Effects of screentime on the health and well-being of children and adolescents: a systematic review of reviews. *British Medical Journal.* 3 January, 2019; 9(1). https://bmjopen.bmj.com/content/9/1/e023191

16 Sara Novak. Investigating screen time's impact on the attention span. *Discovery Magazine.* 10 December, 2021. www.discovermagazine.com/mind/investigating-screen-times-impact-on-the-attention-span

17 MCHC Health Matters. *Excessive Screen Time Linked to Anxiety, Depression, ADHD, and Obesity in Children.* 15 April, 2018. https://mchcinc.org/health-matters-news/health-matters-excessive-screen-time-linked-to-anxiety-depression-adhd-and-obesity-in-children

18 MCHC Health Matters. *Excessive Screen Time Linked to Anxiety, Depression, ADHD, and Obesity in Children.* 15 April, 2018. https://mchcinc.org/health-matters-news/health-matters-excessive-screen-time-linked-to-anxiety-depression-adhd-and-obesity-in-children

19 Perri Klass. *Boredom.* Harvard Medicine Journal. https://hms.harvard.edu/magazine/adventure-issue/boredom

20 Savvy Cyber Kids: Educating & Empowering Digital Citizens. *Why are screens so addictive?* https://savvycyberkids.org/2021/01/13/why-are-screens-so-addictive

21 Brigitte Granger. *Why Rewards Are Destroying Your Motivation.* www.getsupporti.com/post/intrinsic-motivation

22 Gary Wilson. *The Great Porn Experiment.* TEDxGlasgow. 2012. www.youtube.com/watch?v=wSF82AwSDiU

23 Children's and teenage books on sex education and the facts of life (Waterstone's list). www.waterstones.com/category/childrens-teenage/personal-and-social-issues/body-and-health/sex-education-and-the-facts-of-life

24 Edward L. Deci and Richard M. Ryan. *Intrinsic Motivation and Self-Determination in Human Behavior.* Springer; 1985. https://link.springer.com/book/10.1007/978-1-4899-2271-7

25 Dinah Murray, Mike Lesser, and Wendy Lawson. Attention, monotropism and the diagnostic criteria for Autism. *Autism.* 1 May 2005; 9(2). https://web.archive.org/web/20180519194244/http://www.autismusundcomputer.de/english/139.pdf

26 Ibraheem Rehman, Navid Mahabadi, Terrence Sanvictores, and Chaudhry I. Rehman. Classical conditioning. *Stat-Pearls*. 2023. https://pubmed.ncbi.nlm.nih.gov/29262194

27 Dogs for Good (Registered Charity). *Autism assistance dogs for children*. www.dogsforgood.org/how-we-help/assistance-dog/autism-assistance-dogs-children

28 Adele Faber and Elaine Mazlish. *How to Talk so Kids Will Listen and Listen so Kids Will Talk*. Piccadilly Press; 2017.

29 Katy Elphinstone. 'Kids these days. I blame the parents!' July 2017. www.neurofabulous.org.uk/article-parent-blaming.html

30 Susan Cain. *The Power of Introverts*. www.ted.com/talks/susan_cain_the_power_of_introverts/c

31 Nina S. Mounts and Jaipaul L. Roopnarine. Social-cognitive play patterns in same-age and mixed-age preschool classrooms. *American Educational Research Journal*. September 1987; 24(3). https://journals.sagepub.com/doi/abs/10.3102/00028312024003463

32 Dr Damian Milton. *The Double Empathy Problem*. 2 March, 2018. www.autism.org.uk/advice-and-guidance/professional-practice/double-empathy; The Autistic Advocate. *An Introduction to the Double Empathy Problem* (short video). 2022. www.youtube.com/watch?v=qpXwYD9bGyU

33 Melanie Parker. *The Desire for Friendship Runs Deeper in Primates Than We Thought*. 16 February, 2020. www.primaterescue.org/the-desire-for-friendship-runs-deeper-in-primates-than-we-thought

34 Mona Delahooke. *Beyond Behaviors: Using Brain Science and Compassion to Understand and Solve Children's Behavioral Challenges*. PESI Publishing; 1st edition, 2019.

35 Mike McRae. *For Those with Autism, Eye Contact Isn't Just Weird, It's Distressing*. 21 June, 2017. www.sciencealert.com/for-those-with-autism-eye-contact-isn-t-just-weird-it-s-distressing

36 Ralph Savarese. *I Object: Autism, Empathy, and the Trope of Personification*. Emory University. 19 February, 2014. www.youtube.com/watch?v=uZxfeA8thjc

37 Yvette Brend. *Cuteness power: Why watching animal videos is good for your brain.* CBC News. 30 April, 2017. www.cbc.ca/news/canada/british-columbia/cuteness-cute-kawaii-power-krigolso-uvic-joshua-dale-japan-1.3984970

38 Vikram K. Jaswal, Allison Wayne, and Hudson Golino. Eye-tracking reveals agency in assisted autistic communication. *Scientific Reports.* 12 May, 2020. 10(7882). www.nature.com/articles/s41598-020-64553-9

39 Donald N. Cardinal and Mary A. Falvey. The maturing of facilitated communication: a means toward independent communication. *Research and Practice for Persons with Severe Disabilities.* January 2015; 39(3): 189–194. www.researchgate.net/publication/272957524_The_Maturing_of_Facilitated_Communication_A_Means_Toward_Independent_Communication

40 Danya Ruttenberg. *On Repentance and Repair: Making Amends in an Unapologetic World.* Beacon Press; 13 September, 2022.

41 Adele Faber and Elaine Mazlish. *How to Talk So Kids Will Listen and Listen So Kids Will Talk.* Piccadilly Press; 2017.

42 Katy Elphinstone. *Twenty-four fabulous & socially acceptable ways to shut people down.* March 2023. www.neurofabulous.org.uk/article-tips-on-shutting-people-down.html

43 Alfie Kohn. *Punished by Rewards: The Trouble with Gold Stars, Incentive Plans, A's, Praise, and Other Bribes.* Houghton Mifflin; 2018. www.alfiekohn.org/punished-rewards/

44 Katy Elphinstone. *Should I praise my child? A fresh perspective.* www.neurofabulous.org.uk/praising-children.html

45 differentnotdeficient. *What is Pathological Demand Avoidance (PDA)?* Neuroclastic. 27 August, 2019. https://neuroclastic.com/what-is-pathological-demand-avoidance-pda

46 bell hooks. *Teaching to Transgress: Education as the Practice of Freedom.* Routledge; 1994.

47 Oolong. *Autistic Skill Sets: A Spiky Profile of Peaks and Troughs.* Neuroclastic. 5 July, 2019. https://neuroclastic.com/autistic-skill-sets

48 Carla Hannaford. *Smart Moves*. Great Ocean Publishers; 2nd edition, 2005.

49 Shiori Zinnen. *Listen and learn: How audiobooks can support literacy development*. Reading Partners. 17 October, 2021. https://readingpartners.org/blog/audiobooks

50 Alfie Kohn. *No Contest: The Case Against Competition. Why we lose in our race to win*. Houghton Mifflin; 2nd edition, 1992.

51 Catherine Holecko. *Non-Competitive Active Games for Kids*. Verywell Family. 9 May, 2020. www.verywellfamily.com/non-competitive-games-for-kids-1257352

52 How to get occupational therapy (UK): www.nhs.uk/conditions/occupational-therapy; Find Occupational Therapists near me (US): www.healthgrades.com/occupational-therapy-directory/occupational-therapy

53 Not Fine in School. *DfE Clarification of Legislative Expectations*. https://notfineinschool.co.uk/nfis-resources (This outlines expectations in the UK in relation to authorizing absence from school, and alternative provision if children are unable to attend school.)

54 Not Fine in School. *DfE Clarification of Legislative Expectations*. https://notfineinschool.co.uk/nfis-resources (This outlines expectations in the UK in relation to authorizing absence from school, and alternative provision if children are unable to attend school.)

55 Robin L. O'Grady and Nicole Matthews-Creech. *Why Children Don't Tell*. 2017. https://lacasacenter.org/why-child-abuse-victims-dont-tell/

56 Sociocracy For All: Sociocracy in Classrooms and Student Councils (For Teachers): www.sociocracyforall.org/sociocracy-in-schools-for-teachers

57 Naomi Fisher. *Changing Our Minds: How Children Can Take Control of Their Own Learning*. Robinson; 2021.

58 Eating Disorders Victoria. *Eating Disorders and Autism*. www.eatingdisorders.org.au/eating-disorders-a-z/eating-disorders-and-autism

59 Sheryl Ankrom. *Anxiety and GI Issues: What's the Connection?*.

VeryWell Mind. 21 April, 2023. www.verywellmind.com/gastrointestinal-gi-symptoms-and-anxiety-disorders-2584240

60 Moneek Madra, Roey Ringel, and Kara G. Margolis. Gastrointestinal issues and Autism Spectrum Disorder. *Child and Adolescent Psychiatric Clinics of North America*. 2 April, 2020; 29(3): 501–513. www.ncbi.nlm.nih.gov/pmc/articles/PMC8608248

61 Harvard School of Health. *The Nutrition Source: The Microbiome*. www.hsph.harvard.edu/nutritionsource/microbiome/#role-probiotics

62 Children's and teenage books on sex education and the facts of life (Waterstone's list). www.waterstones.com/category/childrens-teenage/personal-and-social-issues/body-and-health/sex-education-and-the-facts-of-life; Susie Day. LGBTQ books for children aged 8–12. Book-Trust. 13 February, 2018. www.booktrust.org.uk/news-and-features/features/2018/february/lgbtq-books-for-children-aged-8-12

63 Bladder & Bowel UK. *Understanding Why Some Children Smear Poo: A guide for parents and carers*. 2020. www.bbuk.org.uk/wp-content/uploads/2020/09/Understanding-Why-Some-Children-Smear-Poo.pdf

64 Helen Dolphin. RADAR Keys explained: What are they, where can I use them and how do I get one? (for use of disabled toilets). 2020. https://news.motability.co.uk/everyday-tips/radar-keys-explained-what-are-they-where-can-i-use-them-and-how-do-i-get-one

65 Neuroclastic. *What is ABA?* https://neuroclastic.com/what-is-aba

66 Ella Lobregt-van Buuren, Marjolijn Hoekert, Bram Sizoo, and Andreas M. Grabrucker. Autism, adverse events, and trauma. *Autism Spectrum Disorders* [Internet]. 20 August, 2021. https://pubmed.ncbi.nlm.nih.gov/34495617

67 Dr Damian Milton. *The Double Empathy Problem*. 2 March, 2018. www.autism.org.uk/advice-and-guidance/professional-practice/double-empathy

68 Meghan Ashburn. *Before You Start Grieving for Your Autistic Child...* Not An Autism Mom. 24 October, 2019. https://notanautismmom.com/2019/10/24/grieving-autism

69 Luna Rose. *How to Be Ready for an Autism Assessment.* 14 May, 2023. www.wikihow.com/Be-Ready-for-an-Autism-Assessment

70 Jessica Flynn. *Why Autism Functioning Labels Are Harmful – and What to Say Instead.* The Mighty. 23 July, 2018. https://themighty.com/topic/autism-spectrum-disorder/autism-functioning-labels-low-functioning-high-functioning

71 Kamila Markram and Henry Markram. The Intense World Theory: a unifying theory of the neurobiology of autism. *Frontiers in Human Neuroscience.* 21 December, 2010; 4: 224. www.ncbi.nlm.nih.gov/pmc/articles/PMC3010743

72 Albertyna Paciorek and Lina Skora. Vagus nerve stimulation as a gateway to interoception. *Frontiers in Psychology.* 29 July, 2020; 11:1659. https://pubmed.ncbi.nlm.nih.gov/32849014

73 Bessel van der Kolk. *The Body Keeps the Score: Brain, Mind, and Body in the Healing of Trauma.* Penguin Publishing Group; 2015.

74 Nishat Choudhury. *Nine out of ten autistic women are victims of sexual assault – WHO study reveals.* 28 April, 2022. www.openaccessgovernment.org/nine-out-of-ten-autistic-women-are-victims-of-sexual-assault/134603

75 Devon Price. *Unmasking Autism: The Power of Embracing Our Hidden Neurodiversity.* Monoray; 1st edition, 2022.

76 Tara Brach. *Radical Compassion: Learning to Love Yourself and Your World through the Practice of RAIN.* Rider. 2020.

77 Lauri Nummenmaa, Enrico Glerean, Riitta Hari, and Jari K. Hietanen. Bodily maps of emotions. *Proceedings of the National Academy of Sciences (PNAS).* December 2013; 111(2): 646–651. www.pnas.org/doi/10.1073/pnas.1321664111

78 Kieran Rose. *Autistic Masking and Autistic Burnout.* The Autistic Advocate. https://theautisticadvocate.com/autistic-masking

79 Helen Edgar. *Supporting Children through Autistic Burnout (Parent/Carer Guide).* Autistic Realms. 5 December, 2022. www.autisticrealms.com/post/supporting-children-through-autistic-burnout-parents-guide

80 Gabor Maté. *Good People Tend to Die Young.* www.youtube.com/watch?v=uLEUT8aBokY

81 Cheryl Platzman Weinstock. *The hidden danger of suicide in autism.* Spectrum. 8 August, 2018. www.spectrumnews.org/features/deep-dive/hidden-danger-suicide-autism

82 Wikipedia. *Spoon theory.* https://en.wikipedia.org/wiki/Spoon_theory

83 Peter Levine. *Waking the Tiger: Healing Trauma.* North Atlantic Books; 1997.

84 Micah O. Mazurek and Gregory F. Petroski. Sleep problems in children with autism spectrum disorder: examining the contributions of sensory over-responsivity and anxiety. *Sleep Medicine.* February 2015; 16(2): 270–9. https://pubmed.ncbi.nlm.nih.gov/25600781